Crossroads

Crossroads

by
Leon
Jaworski

with
Dick Schneider

David C. Cook Publishing Co.
ELGIN, ILLINOIS—WESTON, ONTARIO

CROSSROADS

Library of Congress Cataloging in Publication Data

Jaworski, Leon.
       Crossroads.

1.   Jaworski, Leon.   2. Lawyers—United States—Biography.
I. Schneider, Dick, 1923-   joint author.
II. Title
KF373.J38A34   349.73'092'4   [B]   80-51272
                                              AACR1
ISBN 0-89191-289-4

FIRST EDITION
February, 1981

ISBN 0-89191-289-4

LC 80-51272

To Jeannette
For faith and prayer

Contents

Acknowledgments

The idea of writing a book reflecting my Christian convictions and the part they played in the course of my major endeavors had crossed my mind from time to time in recent years. Each occasion passed without a decision until several persons squarely confronted me on this very subject. After much thought, I felt inspired to proceed with the venture.

It goes almost without saying that much is owed to all of the pastors who have been my good shepherds in the course of my life, beginning with my father and continuing down to my present pastor, Dr. J. W. Lancaster. I must not fail to include other ministers, priests, and rabbis with whom I have had both social and spiritual contact through the years and whom I number among my good friends.

Jeannette and our children, Joanie, Claire, and Joseph have been most helpful. For highly valued secretarial assistance, I am grateful to Camille Crews.

Preface

A few words are necessary to offset any possible interpretation that this volume is written in a pharisaical aura. There is not the slightest intent to separate myself from my fellow sinners.

This effort is just the contrary. Although it is not a public washing of wrongs and sins, it is not designed to deny them. It is designed to reveal how, despite his sins, a believer in Christ finds guidance and strength to meet the crossroads of life.

Throughout my life I have considered the communications between my God and myself to be personal, and I have treated them as privileged. I have never chosen to speak of them in public. But the impact of my experiences of the power of God through Jesus Christ and how his guiding hand was felt in my severest travails are matters I am now prepared to acknowledge to the Lord's glory. If their recounting is of help to my fellowman, I shall feel greatly rewarded.

1
The Man
in the Front Pew

A cold breeze blew newpapers down the avenue and snapped at our coats as my wife and I climbed the steep steps leading into the New York Avenue Presbyterian Church that Sunday morning. It was February 10, 1974.

Jeannette and I had been worshiping at this church since she had joined me in Washington, where I was serving as special prosecutor on the Watergate case. This capital-city landmark was only a fifteen-minute walk from the Jefferson Hotel, in which we had an apartment. We both enjoyed the brisk walk.

After Houston's mild climate we were still not accustomed to Washington winters, so it was good to step into the warm vestibule.

But even before we removed our coats I sensed that something unusual was happening. There was an electricity in the air. My feeling was confirmed when an usher in a dark blue suit hurried up to us, his face brimming with excitement.

"Good morning, Mr. and Mrs. Jaworski," he beamed. His voice dropped an octave. "The president will be worshiping with us this morning."

Jeannette and I glanced at each other as the usher led us down the blue-carpeted aisle to one of the white pews.

Why? I wondered as I settled on the cushions and stared unseeingly at the program in my hand. It wasn't often that President Nixon attended church services outside of the White House. Whatever his reason, it was obvious that he was coming. I could see Secret Service men quietly stationing themselves in unobtrusive locations, their eyes constantly roving the sanctuary.

Strains from the organ's prelude filled the air, and the sun briefly broke through the overcast sky, illuminating the beautiful stained-glass windows.

Focusing on the program, I saw that the minister, Dr. George M. Docherty, would be speaking on "What Happened to Courage?" How much I needed this resource, I thought. I had come to Washington confident that I could meet the challenge, but an unexpected discovery had severely shaken me.

Jeannette nudged me and I looked up; a low rustle filled the air and heads turned to watch the presidential party enter the sanctuary. Richard Nixon walked down the aisle with firm step, head high, shoulders slightly hunched with that familiar aplomb. His party was led to two pews that had been kept open in the front of the church. It was the first time I had seen the president since coming to Washington. Neither of us had gone out of his way to see the other.

The dignified tones of the organ led into the processional hymn, "Onward, Christian Soldiers," and Jeannette and I stood up with our hymnals in our hands. But I could not concentrate on the words. My mind went back to November when at the urging of the White House chief of staff, General Alexander Haig, I had agreed to come to the capital to take on the special prosecutor's responsibilities.

I had come believing that the president was innocent of any wrongdoing. Overeager men on his staff, I felt, had been responsible for the break-in and the nefarious cover-up attempts.

Then in December, 1973, I was stunned as I listened to a tape recording made on March 21, 1973, of an animated conversation between President Nixon, his chief of staff, Bob Haldeman, and counsel John Dean. In that unmistakable voice I heard Nixon conspiring to suppress the truth about the Watergate burglary by providing hush money to the burglars. I listened to him coaching his chief of staff on how to testify untruthfully to a grand jury and still avoid a charge of perjury. It was like an unexpected blow to my solar plexus.

I realized then for the first time what a torturous and agonizing road lay ahead for me and the whole country. As yet, only a few people knew of this tape. And now the man who had spoken those condemning words stood just a short distance from me in an attitude of worship.

I thought of another president, Abraham Lincoln, who had worshiped at this church. He had also suffered the scorn of many—but for vastly different reasons.

Questions swirled through my mind as I gazed at the familiar profile. Why was he here? Was he sincere? Did he feel he needed the prayers of others? Was he laying his problems before the Lord?

As the organ swelled and hundreds of voices filled the air, a picture appeared before my mind, a picture born of wishful thinking. I saw the president stepping to the front of the church as the hymn ended. I saw him face the congregation and say, "I want to say in the presence of God and all of you that I have been guilty of wrongdoing. I have made some grievous mistakes and admit this before you, our nation, and the world. I ask for your forgiveness."

As this wild and improbable vision hung before me I knew instinctively that the nation would accept his apology. Some would continue to denounce him, but the majority of the people would see that this man was big enough and honorable enough to admit his guilt. And in a spirit of compassion they would forgive him.

The reverberating finale of the hymn brought me back to reality. How ridiculous to even imagine such a thing! The man in the dark suit in the front pew would no more walk out of his pew than become a monk.

Someone began reading the Old Testament Scripture lesson. It was from Isaiah 41:1-10, and I caught the words "Come now and speak. The court is ready for your case. . . ."

The case, I thought; it was certainly building to a complicated tangle because of the deviousness of this man. Again his voice on the tape echoed in my memory. How could he speak in such despicable terms, using the Lord's name in vain as he did, and still face his Maker?

Later we rose to sing another hymn, "Lord, for the Mercies of This Night." Mercy. The word stirred me. As the music surged I looked up to the rose and violet stained-glass window and envisioned the figure of Christ standing before us, his hands outstretched. "Come unto me, all ye that labour and are heavy laden. . . ."

Indeed I was heavy laden. But was he, that man in the front pew who now lifted his head to sing? Of course he must be, I had to admit. Richard Milhous Nixon stood before Christ just as I did, the Christ whose hands were outstretched to us all. I had to accept that.

I, too, was a sinner. And in no way had I any right to judge this man's relationship to God. That was something between him and the Lord.

I silently asked God to forgive me for judging another man's relationship to him. As I did so a heaviness seemed to lift from my mind, and a sense of peace began to fill me. I felt I had come to a crossroads, the first of many that I would face in the twisting route of Watergate. This time I again seemed to have taken the right turn. For I knew that I could not journey through this crucible of anguish in a spirit of recrimination, prejudice, or vengeance. It would have to be traveled purely in a search for truth so that right would prevail—not only for the people of the United States but also for this man in the front pew.

As I settled back in my seat I thought of the many other crossroads I had faced in my sixty-eight years, the agonizing decisions made, and the heartbreaking lessons I had learned. My mind drifted back to the little Texas prairie town in which I faced the first crossroad that would affect my life forever.

2
Heritage

It was evening in the little cemetery set amidst undulating Texas farmland. A whippoorwill called from a tall cedar, and a giant orange sun burned near the hazy horizon. As a nine year old, I had come to Lone Oak Cemetery with my father, two older brothers, and a little sister to say good-bye to our mother.

It was August, 1914, and we were leaving our little town of Geronimo the next morning to move to the big city of Waco. The five of us had walked across the dusty road from the parsonage to visit our mother's grave one more time. I studied its little headstone bearing her name, Marie Mira Jaworski, and the dates of her birth and death. Nearby stood a large granite cross bearing the German words *Die Liebe Höret Nimmer Auf.*

Love never ends read the inscription, which I knew was

inspired by a Bible verse. I also knew it reflected papa's deep feelings for this loved one who had died shortly after my sister was born. His eyes misting, papa leaned down to straighten the glass-encased floral wreath that mama's parents had sent all the way from Vienna, Austria.

I felt his strong hand on my shoulder as he drew us around him for prayer. In his deep baritone German he thanked God for mama and all of us and asked for protection and blessings on our coming journey.

As he prayed I remembered his teaching us that none of the good things we try to do will last. Only the love we give others for the sake of God endures forever.

Shadows from the cedars edged across mama's grave, and I looked over to the giant oak in the middle of the cemetery and wondered. Was *maminka*, as papa called her, watching us from heaven? Papa said she did. Then she, too, knew we were moving away.

I had never really known her. She had died at age thirty-five, when I was three. All I could remember was a coffin in the darkened parlor and grown-ups shushing me in the kitchen. Her picture had hung in that parlor later, and I would often study her gentle face with its soft, sweet smile.

Mama was a pretty Viennese woman who had met my father, Joseph Jaworski, when he was a young minister in Europe. By then father was a Latin scholar, fluent in several languages, having studied at a seminary and universities in Germany and Austria. Born in Crakow, Poland, he had migrated to Germany where he became an evangelical pastor. There he met my mother.

They fell in love, she with the stalwart, dark-haired man with a black mustache and burning brown eyes; he with the slim, attractive Marie who wore her brunette hair in an upswept pompadour.

Two sons—Joseph, Jr., and Hannibal—were born in Germany. However, father chafed at the prospect of raising them in a continent dominated by royalty, a land in which one's life seemed regimented from birth. He had heard of a country in which every man was free to seek his own destiny and worship God as he chose.

But he could hardly bring himself to leave both his and Marie's family: they might never see them again. He would also be giving up a prestigious position as a cleric.

Yet something far beyond family and position and material goods drew Joseph Jaworski to leave his adopted homeland: his vision of a land that still seemed to be in submission to God, a land where every man was guaranteed the right to life, liberty, and the pursuit of happiness.

He took his Marie and two baby sons and boarded a steamship for the United States in 1903. Somewhere he had heard of German-speaking settlements in central Texas. It seemed best to make his transition to American life there. So when the little family emerged from Ellis Island in New York harbor, father bought railroad tickets for Texas.

After a year's stay in Coupland, a small community near Austin, he moved his family to Waco, a young city still bustling with pioneer spirit. Father was welcomed as a pastor of the Evangelical Zion's Church at 627 South Eighth Street. At the same time he was beginning a deep, lifelong love affair with his new homeland.

In 1905 I was born, and my sister, Mary, a dollish child, followed a year later. Soon mother's health began to fail, and her doctor recommended that father take her to a rural area where she could have more rest and quiet. Father heard of an opening in a small evangelical church in the hamlet of Geronimo in Guadalupe County, which was located in southern Texas. After he met with its congregation, they liked the earnest young preacher and asked him to be their pastor.

We soon moved into the little, white frame parsonage near the red brick church. The house had an old-fashioned open well in the kitchen. Outside under cedars and chinaberry trees, chickens and turkeys clucked and gobbled around the yard. But, despite the peaceful surroundings, mother continued to weaken until one day father found himself alone with four little children.

Yet mother's presence remained with our close-knit family. Heaven, as father often pointed out in his sermons, was closer than the person next to us in the pew, even more real than the walls of the church surrounding us. "If it were not so, I would have told you," he would say, reading Jesus' words from the Bible.

But father did more than illuminate the teachings of Christ from the pulpit. He had a way of instilling the presence of God into our daily lives. One Sunday afternoon after giving the blessing at dinner, he looked seriously at the four of us and said, "I have something to say to you, *kinder*."

My spine stiffened. When no one was around, I had been using my air rifle to shoot at the shiny metal ball mounted near the top of the church's soaring steeple. I had thrilled at the satisfying *plink* of a well-aimed pellet. Had God told father about this?

God hadn't. Father went on to point out that some of us had been misbehaving in Sunday school. "How often must I tell you," he said, "that the pastor's children must set a good example?

"Remember," he added quietly, "*maminka* is watching."

All of us dutifully promised to behave better, though an admonition heeded in his presence was not so closely observed in his absence.

Often father would be gone late into the night, sitting at the bedside of a dying parishioner or counseling a bereaved farmer. In his soft German he would help the supplicant see beyond the darkness to the promises of eternal life.

But this did not comfort tiny Mary or me at the age of five as we lay awake longing for the welcoming crunch of his buggy wheels on the gravel. Our nearest neighbor lived over a mile away. Night winds moaned in the cedars in the front yard, and I would shiver at the wail of coyotes in the mesquite groves that stretched endlessly outside our bedroom window.

Then a form would appear at my side and I'd feel the comforting pressure of my ten-year-old brother, Joseph, sitting on the edge of the mattress.

"Nidi," he would say, "don't worry. We'll be all right; papa will be home soon."

Despite his comforting words, I'd still tremble.

But I always enjoyed accompanying father to the many weddings and baptisms around the countryside. Since most of the local people were of German heritage and followed their ancestral traditions, these were highly festive occasions, with banquet tables piled high with all kinds of delicacies.

"Nidi," father would say, "come along with me today." I would eagerly hold Peter, his horse, while he harnessed it to the gig, a light two-wheeled vehicle. Father would put on his big, panama straw hat, and off we'd go on what was sometimes a half-day journey.

Over the soft *clip-clop* of the horse's hooves and the creaking of the gig, I would besiege papa with questions.

"Why did you name me Leonidas?" I asked one day.

"He was a famous king of ancient Sparta," father answered, flicking the reins. My father was a student of history and frequently referred to events that transpired in ancient Greece and Rome, both in sermons and conversations.

And so as the hours passed my father took me back to 480 B.C. when the Persian king, Xerxes, invaded Greece through the pass at Thermopylae.

Leonidas, he pointed out, held this pass with only three hundred soldiers against the Persian army. He gave his life in the effort.

"Nidi," he added, "courage in life is so very important, courage to do right and to stand up for what is right. Leonidas of Sparta gave his life for what he believed."

A few quiet moments followed as I tried to understand the full meaning of what my father said. He, too, seemed to be contemplating the subject when I turned to him and asked, "And why did you name Hanni, Hannibal?"

He smiled and quickly answered, "Hannibal was a great general and statesman of ancient Carthage. He was known for his leadership abilities. Every country needs good, strong-hearted leaders. America has been blessed with them. Some countries in Europe have not been so fortunate."

At that time World War I was raging in Europe.

Then papa began doing something that puzzled us. It wasn't unusual for him to make afternoon calls on parishioners after church. But to visit the same family every Sunday? We all wondered. The Oelkerses lived a mile down the road, and we knew papa enjoyed talking with Mr. Oelkers about his experiences as a Confederate soldier.

"But you would think they'd have talked everything out," Joseph commented to us younger children one day.

Later that Sunday afternoon papa brought a pretty blonde-haired woman home with him. It was Adele Oelkers, our neighbor's daughter. "You will have a new mother soon," said papa proudly. As we children awkwardly greeted her, she embraced us all with loving arms. A shy, gentle woman, she won our hearts.

With a mother in the home, our usual celebrations of Christmas, Easter, and birthdays became even more festive. As I grew older I would be more and more impressed by how father would express his gratitude to God at these holiday dinners for keeping us children safe and bringing us our new mother.

Hearing and watching papa talk so openly with God as a living presence helped make the Lord even more real to me. By the time I was nine I had an implicit trust in a heavenly Father who knew everything I thought and did—and still loved me beyond any human comprehension.

And so on that August evening in 1914 as we all stood together in the little churchyard in Geronimo, I felt I needed God more than ever. My father's deep baritone voice thanked God for his protection and blessings, and I silently and passionately joined him. I was very afraid of moving to a strange, new city.

3
Ein' Feste Burg Ist Unser Gott

Waco. Its very name of two quick syllables was so unlike Geronimo and another nearby town, New Braunfels, that fitted in with our German pronunciation. When I pronounced it *Vay-coh*, Hannibal and Joseph roared with laughter. "You'll really be in trouble in the new school if you don't learn to speak English correctly," they warned me.

But even my big brothers were wary of the move. Geronimo was the only town we children had known. Visits to the nearby towns of Sequin and New Braunfels had been brief and seldom. We were at home with people who spoke German; father's parishioners had become like family to him. If he hadn't conducted their weddings and funerals, he had baptized and confirmed them.

However, father's former church in Waco, Evangelical Zion's, needed a pastor and had asked him to return. At first

24

he wouldn't think of leaving. But Evangelical Zion's had pressed him all the more, and once he considered the expanded educational opportunities for his children—including Baylor University—he had finally accepted the call.

The trip to Waco was my first train ride. As the engine puffed north across the Texas prairie, cows and calves turned and ran from the smoke and sparks. Peering out the window I felt as if we were headed for another planet.

When we finally arrived and walked out of the Waco station, I was awestruck by the blocks of buildings, which seemed to stretch endlessly down wide streets, teeming with traffic. Then I saw my first policeman, his blue uniform resplendent with brass buttons.

"Watch out, Leon," whispered Hannibal teasingly, "that policeman will catch you and put you in jail."

I believed him implicitly. As the parsonage was not quite ready, we spent our first night in a Waco hotel, with my brothers and me sharing one bed. I hid trembling under the covers, convinced that the policeman was peering at me over the transom!

Waco marked the beginning of a new life for us all. Father's congregation, a mixed group of blue-collar workers with a scattering of successful businessmen of German background, believed in supporting its pastor in every way, and father responded. Under his inspired leadership the thirty-three-year-old church blossomed in growth and activities. The Sunday school attendance mushroomed, the sanctuary was filled every week, and soon the trustees began talking of building a new church.

But I had some personal growing to do, too. Since I had been used to speaking and reading German in Geronimo, I talked with a thick accent and found reading textbooks difficult.

My teacher was a brawny, tough-looking woman. I was immediately afraid of her the first day I walked into her fourth-grade class. Later when she called on me to recite, I found myself so nervous I sometimes responded in German. The other children thought this quite funny. Their laughter rang unmercifully in my ears.

My first examination paper was a disaster. The teacher had passed out the tests, and while the other students busily scribbled answers, I sat staring at the paper, stricken.

I couldn't read all the questions.

Finally I broke down sobbing.

The teacher stepped down the aisle to me, "What's wrong, Leonidas?"

I looked up quavering, then between sobs explained my problem. Instead of showing impatience, the tall, raw-boned woman bent down and carefully explained the questions.

"Now don't you worry, son," she said comfortingly. "Even if you miss some, I know you always study hard."

Her compassion restored my confidence, and as weeks passed I soon began to master English.

But that didn't prevent my classmates from making fun of my name.

One night I dragged into the parlor where papa was reading his Bible. "Papa."

He looked up, taking off his silver-rimmed glasses. "Yes, Nidi?"

"I wish we could change our name."

"But why?"

"The others tease me."

Father stood up and put his hand on my shoulder. "Nidi," he said gently, "what's in a name?"

He looked at me through understanding eyes. "What really counts in life is what you are, what you accomplish," he said. "That is what the world will remember you by, not your name."

He pointed out that children were prone to make fun of anything they didn't understand. "When one doesn't know any better," he added, "the unfamiliar is feared, and that is usually expressed in ridicule."

"This applies to a lot of adults, too," he added sadly.

After papa's explanation the name calling didn't bother me as much.

I continued to study as hard as ever, for the idea of failure was completely unacceptable, mainly because we knew that papa and mother would be so disappointed.

Papa always stressed perfection in everything we did. He would carefully examine our text papers and study our grade reports, clucking his tongue over anything he felt hadn't measured up. Doing well at our school assignments was something to be expected, and in earlier years he had often helped us with our homework late into the night by the light of the flickering kerosene lamp. I also continued to feel that somewhere up in heaven mama was watching us, too.

By the time I was in seventh grade I was doing well. One day my teacher passed out our grade cards, and I was thrilled to see that I had top grades in every subject. The teacher, probably feeling that I still needed a dose of self-confidence, mentioned to the class how well I had done.

My head suddenly swelling, I stood up and made a big bow.

"And *that*, Leonidas," she quickly added, "takes off on your deportment."

But any cockiness that may have developed within me was soon shaken. By 1917 America had entered World War I. In the hysteria of the times anything German suddenly became anathema. Sauerkraut was called "liberty cabbage," and many cities with streets such as Wagner Avenue and Beethoven Drive quickly changed them to Pershing Avenue and Wilson Drive.

One evening father came home for dinner in a somber mood. After he had said the grace, he told us what had happened that afternoon on Main Street. "You may be hearing about it and that's why I'm telling you," he said. "But please don't be upset."

As he was crossing a busy corner a man had rushed up and struck him on the face, cursing and shouting, "You dirty Hun!" Father, a gymnast in his youth, was able to restrain the man until a policeman came up to arrest him.

"I think he had been drinking," father said sadly as he carved the meat, "or he may have something wrong with his mind.

"At least," he looked up, "he is certainly not representative of the people in Waco."

But I was uneasy, all the same. Father was a man who was never afraid of anything. I had already heard much about the hatred and anger directed at our enemy across the sea and had seen war posters showing men in spiked helmets bayoneting children.

Father's church, Evangelical Zion's, sang hymns in German. And father saw no reason to change that, especially since many young doughboys of German descent from nearby Camp MacArthur were flocking to his church. They were mostly from southeastern Wisconsin and southwestern Michigan and appreciated services like those at home. Father wanted to do all he could for them, knowing with a heavy heart that many would soon be in combat overseas.

But no one knew that one Sunday a person who was suspicious of anything German walked by the church as the congregation was singing Martin Luther's famous hymn "A Mighty Fortress Is Our God." The church had opened all its windows to catch any stray breeze in the heat of that Texas summer. The congregation was singing in German, and the opening words *Ein' feste burg ist unser Gott* drifted out. The listener thought he heard something else, and lost no time in getting in touch with the federal authorities.

Next Sunday father came home from church as usual, still wearing his black vestments and dripping with perspiration. He sank down at the kitchen table with a sigh, looking up at mother gratefully as she handed him a cold glass of lemonade, his favorite drink.

"Well," he said, leaning back, "let me tell you about our visitor this morning."

Father had stood at the door to visit with his parishioners as usual when a stranger in a dark suit had come up to him.

Father extended his hand to greet the visitor. "Good morning, sir," he said, striking up a conversation. "Do you live in Waco?"

"No, I'm just here visiting," he answered. "Thought I'd like to take in one of your services."

Father and the stranger had seemed to hit it off, for they were soon engaged in easy conversation. Finally, the man, obviously embarrassed, said, "Reverend Jaworski, I must tell you why I'm here. I'm a United States government agent. Because I speak German I was sent to check out your services."

After apologizing for intruding, he said, "Someone reported that you were all engaged in seditious activities, because he heard your people singing *Hindenberg ist unser Gott*. As you know Hindenberg is the leader of the German forces."

Father drained his lemonade glass, leaned back in his chair, and shook his head in disbelief.

In a sense the incident was laughable—yet also frightening to us. As I sat there watching father across the table I suddenly realized what a load he had to carry on his shoulders, not only now but all the preceding years: raising a family alone, finding a new mother for us, and settling our family in a new city. Now his services were being investigated by the United States government.

I continued to learn from my father as the years passed. Despite his extensive education, he had a facility for speaking the common man's language, enabling his listeners to apply Jesus' teachings to their everyday lives.

Perhaps studying his carefully prepared sermons sparked my interest in forensics. I had already begun taking part in school debates, and by age fourteen was selected as the best debater in Waco High. A year later I went to Houston to take part in a debate before a large audience.

The subject was whether or not our country's immigration laws should be tightened. We drew lots to see which side we'd support, and I found myself arguing for the proposal. My side won the debate. Afterward I wondered, Would my parents have been allowed to enter this country if my debate arguments had been put into effect? Quickly I reminded myself that I had been engaged in debating exercises only. My arguments did not necessarily reflect my personal views. Little did I realize that in the practice of law I would be called upon to defend the rights of an accused, regardless of my opinion or knowledge as to the person's guilt.

Encouraged by my success in this field, and attracted by the challenge of defending the rights of others in a free society, I decided to become a lawyer. Such an endeavor would contribute to the system of government of a country I had come to love and honor.

I set nearby Baylor University as my goal: I could walk to classes and live at home, a very important economic factor. By taking extra high school courses and attending school through one summer, I graduated from high school in three years. Then I took a five-week summer course in shorthand and typing at a local business college so I could work as a stenographer while attending Baylor.

In the meantime, my sister and brothers had been pursuing their particular talents. My blond, blue-eyed brother Joseph had graduated from Baylor and was attending the University of Texas, earning an electrical engineering degree. Hannibal, whom we called "Hanni," was working his way through medical school, and my sister, Mary, who had become very talented in piano, was studying music.

I had little social life as a sixteen-year-old Baylor freshman. Besides studies, my time was taken by working in various professors' offices, in return for a small freshman scholarship given because my father was a clergyman.

But as I walked to and from school I enjoyed some good conversations with my friend Bernard, a Jewish student. Because of our friendship and also, I'm sure, because of my last name, I felt other students thought I was Jewish, too. But this never bothered me. Father had always said to look into a man's heart instead of his race or religion. Bernard had a good heart.

As far as the Baylor coeds were concerned, I might as well have been in knee pants. With my muffin face I looked even younger than my age. Still I had the friendship of my sister. Through the years we had become quite close, since we were only a year apart. Because I enjoyed singing popular songs, on many nights Mary played the piano in our parlor while I went through a whole stack of sheet music.

Once Mary invited me to play tennis with her and her close friend, Jeannette Adam, a dark-haired, brown-eyed attractive girl whose family attended our church. But even then dating was far from my mind.

Girls aside, however, I did my best to become a regular fellow at Baylor. After a few semesters I became active in several campus organizations.

I became involved in other things, too.

One day between classes a friend motioned me around the corner of a building. After glancing about, he furtively pulled a bottle of amber liquid from underneath his coat. "Great stuff," he said, offering it to me. "It just came in."

"What is it?"

"Corn whiskey."

Not wanting to be different, I lifted the bottle to my mouth and found myself coughing and sputtering. It was like liquid lye.

"Sure is . . . good," I gasped.

Next I tried to emulate our dean who chewed tobacco. Our law library was in a nineteenth-century residential building, which served as Baylor's law school in those days. It was here that I learned about Plowboy's Best. After I had unwrapped a square of this pressed tobacco product, I arranged my books, and then took a large bite of it. The wad in my mouth seemed to swell to the size of a baseball. My eyes must have bulged for my study mate said, "What on earth is the matter, Leon? You don't look well."

I certainly didn't feel well. In another few seconds I broke the library's silence as I stampeded outside into some bushes where I lost the tobacco and that day's intake of food.

Giving up chewing tobacco was easy. So I thought I would try nickel cigars. I smoked one walking home from school one afternoon, but I soon wondered if I was going to make it to the house. The telephone poles lining the street seemed to reach for me and the sidewalk began to wobble.

I was careful not to practice such indiscretions in front of my father, who had long ago given up smoking. He had always lectured us boys on the body being the temple of the Holy Spirit. In no way were we to desecrate it. Judging from what had happened every time I tried some kind of tobacco, I began to see his point.

At the same time I was experimenting with a little different life-style, I was also testing new philosophies. In particular I became fascinated by two noted men who did not believe in God: Clarence Darrow, one of the finest trial lawyers of all time, and Robert Ingersoll, the nation's greatest orator of the nineteenth century. I was impressed by Darrow's stubborn and able courtroom defense tactics, and by Ingersoll's beautifully worded orations. Both of them had made great contributions to society.

And yet as I learned more about these two men and dug deeper into history, I realized how unfulfilling their lives had been because of their lack of faith in God. I wondered about Darrow's ultimate beliefs; surely, such a brilliant man would have realized that this life is but a prelude to something far greater.

And despite Ingersoll's beautiful adornments of rhetoric, his words in the end seemed empty, without any real foundation of strength.

I found myself comparing these two men to my father, who, even though he did not possess their eloquence, had something I believed was more vital: a God who gave him solace and strength and the promise of life after death. In the end I felt his kind of faith would give one a far deeper satisfaction than the fame Ingersoll or Darrow had attained.

My father had taught me early in life that material gains do not spell happiness or success, and Baylor's emphasis on

Christian principles and teachings reinforced this belief. But later, when I was beginning law practice, I sometimes wondered how certain individuals whom I met or observed could achieve such great financial and material success and yet so frequently violate Christ's teachings in their daily business and personal lives. As I followed these individuals' careers, I noted that without exception their revels in wealth and apparent happiness were short-lived. There were days of reckoning when this wealth and popularity could no longer sustain them.

It was then I realized that I had forgotten what the Bible taught: "Man looketh on the outward appearance, but the Lord looketh on the heart" (1 Sam. 16:7).

In contrast, I saw the happiness and supreme contentment enjoyed by so many of my friends and acquaintances who had little material gain but whose joy-filled lives exemplified the Bible teaching: "A little that a righteous man hath is better than the riches of many wicked" (Ps. 37:16).

Father's Waco parishioners loved and admired him. One Sunday afternoon the congregation surprised him with a special presentation ceremony in which he was given a shiny black Model T Ford to replace his horse and buggy. Its fittings glinted and its shiny black paint shone in the blazing Texas sun.

I examined it in awe, never having been this close to a motorcar before. "It's wonderful, dad!" I exclaimed, running a hand over an enameled fender.

"Yes," said father, "and you are going to be the chauffeur."

I stared at him.

His answer was quick and decisive. "I don't know how to drive an automobile, and I don't think I ever will."

Every Sunday afternoon when father served a congregation at Riesel, a small town some twenty miles from Waco, I would drive him there. Having already attended morning services, I would take along my homework to complete while father preached.

Our conversations on these trips were not as relaxed as

those in the gig. For now I had to keep an eye out for the horses that shied at our approach, plus be prepared for the fallibilities of the Model T. Once a steering radius rod broke as we turned into Riesel, and we ended up against a telephone pole. Fortunately we had been chugging along rather slowly. Even with such hazards we managed to have good discussions on these trips.

One afternoon as we returned from Riesel I asked father if he had heard the rumor that Ku Klux Klan activities were beginning in our area. During the war some opportunists had revived the supersecret vigilante organization and it seemed to be spreading across the country, both north and south.

"I thought that kind of thing had gone out fifty years ago," I said.

Father shook his head. "Not the evil spirit that is behind such things," he sighed. "Call it the KKK or what have you, there will always be an insidious force—which I believe is of Satan—that makes one group of people think they're better than another, especially when they differ in race and religion.

"You know," he pulled off his panama straw hat to wipe his brow, "when I came to this country I thought I would see the end of such hatred. I felt the United States was inspired into being by God. And yet . . ."

He didn't say anything for a moment as we chugged along the prairie road, the sun sinking behind us. "And yet I'm sure that where God has established something, Satan is right there attempting to destroy it."

"Well," I said, adjusting the spark level as we approached a hill, "perhaps it's all just talk."

"Would to God that it were," he said quietly.

Five months later I was studying my homework when Mary, her brown eyes wide, raced into the room. "Leon," she cried, "come outside!"

I hurried out to the back porch and looked up at a sight that chilled me to the bone.

A fiery cross was flaming angrily in the night, high on a hill a few miles away.

4
The Knights
of the Invisible Empire

The blazing cross had signaled one of the largest gatherings of the Ku Klux Klan in years.

The next day our newspaper, the Waco *News-Tribune*, carried banner headlines: TEN WOUNDED WHEN SHERIFF HALTS KLAN. Through its front-page story I relived the events of the day before.

Telephone wires had crackled earlier that day, Saturday, October 1, 1921, with talk of an impending Klan parade in Lorena, a small town fourteen miles south of Waco. The McLennan County sheriff, Bob Buchanan, found himself in an uncomfortable situation. The law was clear: parading by unknown, masked men was illegal.

I knew what a difficult decision the sheriff must have faced. If he interfered, he would be just one man against a hundred hooded Klansmen and the thousands who were eager to attend the parade. I'm sure he must have wondered if it wouldn't be better to just stay quietly out of the way. After all, the parade wasn't going on outside his office.

But Bob Buchanan vowed to maintain the law, to protect the citizens from the caprice of the Klan, which had spread like wildfire through Texas and the entire country, maiming helpless and innocent people as it went. Women had been carried from their homes and beaten; men flogged until their backs were bloody.

The giant Klan parade was scheduled to begin at 8:30 that night. After an early dinner the McLennan County sheriff with two deputies, M. Burton and Mack Wood, had raced to Lorena in a squad car. The light of torches and flaming crosses illuminated the sky before them.

Sheriff Buchanan confronted the Klan leaders inside their temporary headquarters, a house on the outskirts of town. Outside white-robed figures stood around a huge bonfire, their shadows shifting in the flickering light.

"Parading by masked individuals is against the law," he reminded the two cloaked Klansmen who were in charge. Their eyes peered out at him through slits in their hoods. "If you will just let me see who is leading—so I know who is responsible if anything happens—I will not stop the parade."

Klan members claim that the hood is not worn as a mask to protect them from prosecution but "as a symbol of humility, of anonymity in doing good works." The two leaders argued defiantly for their right to remain unknown.

For almost an hour the sheriff fruitlessly pleaded with them. "Just give me your names," he asked again and again.

Finally he returned to downtown Lorena where he and his deputies paced along the fringe of the teeming sidewalks, shouting for the spectators to disperse. "It is not right for them to pass through here hooded and masked," Buchanan yelled, in order to be heard above the roar of the 3,000 people who lined the length of the main street. "The parade might get out of control. Someone will get hurt."

But excitement and anticipation gripped the onlookers.

Men and women, young children and teenagers milled around the edges of the narrow street, laughing and talking as if they were waiting for a circus to begin. Fathers held tiny tots on their shoulders; babies laughed—or cried—in their mothers' arms.

Some of the spectators were here out of curiosity or to be part of the gala atmosphere. But most citizens of Lorena, Waco, and surrounding communities came to show their support for the Klan; many had openly joined the clandestine organization, others sympathized with it. The mayor of Waco and the Board of Police Commissioners were avowed Klansmen.

Hoots from the crowd protested the sheriff's interference, answering his plea to disband with defiance. Several leading citizens, among them the McLennan County engineer and a local Baptist pastor, tried to "reason" with the sheriff.

But Bob Buchanan stood his ground. "They shan't have the parade," he vowed. "They'll all have to walk over me if they come down the street."

A few brave voices declared that the sheriff was right; he was only doing his duty. But most of the crowd would tolerate no interference. Their howls of protest answered the sheriff's ultimatum. Some zealous people even tried to dissuade Deputy Burton, to weaken the sheriff's meager posse of two.

"I haven't deserted the sheriff before, and I do not intend to leave him now," Burton vowed.

Only a couple of blocks away Klansmen formed into a single column for their march through town. An observer warned the color-bearer: "The sheriff's out to get you. Maybe you'd better stay out of town."

" . . . I'd carry the American flag down the streets of any American city," the Klansman boasted, lifting Old Glory aloft. " 'Fraid to march? Ha!" he shouted. "I followed this old flag against 15,000,000 Germans."

The color-bearer moved forward, flanked by a fellow Klansmen who lifted high a wooden-slatted cross, ablaze with red, electric light bulbs.

The Klan claims that their fiery cross represents "the ideals of Christian civilization." It is not a desecration, according to them, but a symbol of the truth and light of their sacred doctrine: "the blazing spirit of western civilization."

I had seen photographs in recent newspapers of this "blazing spirit" illuminating the bodies of men dangling from trees.

Cheers rang out down the street as the white-clad marchers, swinging into step, began entering town. The applause increased as the parade neared.

Sheriff Buchanan and his two deputies hurried toward the ghostly procession. Just a block from the center of town he confronted the two leaders.

"Parading by masked individuals is against the law," the sheriff shouted. But his words were lost in the noise and hubbub around him. Only the men at the front of the procession heard his order. The flag bearer stopped for a moment. Then he moved forward one step, bringing him face-to-face with the McLennan County sheriff.

Quickly Bob Buchanan reached for the flag-bearer's mask.

With an angry roar the hooded men behind the color guard converged on him. The Klansman with the cross lifted his symbol of "Christian civilization" high and swung it down on the sheriff's head. Bob Buchanan fell to the ground, stunned by the heavy blow.

A pistol shot split the night as spectators and marchers swarmed into a furious melee with cries of "Don't stop that flag!" and "Knock him down!"

Sheriff Buchanan struggled to his feet, drawing a Bowie knife. "Somebody got my gun while I was down!" he shouted to his deputies. Desperately swinging his knife, he cleared a circle around him as fifteen to twenty shots rang out in rapid sequence.

The holiday spirit turned to horror as women screamed and children cried out in bewildered fear. Bullets ricocheted off tin lizzies parked at the curb, exploded plaster on storefronts, and penetrated flesh.

Sheriff Buchanan crumpled to the ground.

During the struggle the American flag dipped only for a moment. Then the original bearer grabbed the colors, the cross bearer joined him, and together they marched on through the crowd. Other Klansmen fell into step, and the line disappeared like phantoms in the night.

For an instant the otherworldly procession held the maddening events in suspension. Then hysteria again roared forth as cries of pain and agony broke the silence. Ten men bleeding from knife or gunshot wounds were helped into nearby drugstores, which had been hurriedly opened for emergency treatment. One of them, Louis Crow, a townsman, would die from a knife wound. He told those who struggled to save his life, "I was just standing beside the road when someone stabbed me. . . . I don't even know who did it." The other injured men, including the sheriff who was struck by two bullets, would recover.

"Jus' tell them that the whitecaps shot me," Sheriff Buchanan gasped to a news reporter. "I begged and I pleaded with them to halt. But they wouldn't hear me."

Twenty-four hours later a lone Klansman was seen posting two, large brown placards around town.

Wife beaters beware—K.K.K. read one. On the other side was the lettering: Crapshooters beware. Our eyes are on you.

The other card carried the inscriptions: Love thy neighbor as theyself, but leave his wife alone. And Chicken thieves look out. We are after you.

The Ku Klux Klan had emerged victorious in its battle with local authorities. Now it was asserting its right to rule.

In the days that followed more signs appeared in Lorena and the surrounding towns, all carrying the same message: The eyes of the Klan are watching you.

As I listened to the excited talk about the riot on Waco streets, I heard a number of people condemn the sheriff for "interfering with something that wasn't his business." Three hundred leading citizens of Lorena signed a public resolution exonerating the Ku Klux Klan from blame and calling for a grand jury probe into the actions of Sheriff Buchanan.

The grand jury hearing was scheduled immediately and over one hundred witnesses testified between October 12 and October 21. On November 5, the grand jury returned a verdict of "no bill." The case was closed. But the Klan-controlled jury did "condemn the methods employed by Sheriff Buchanan and Deputy Sheriff Burton in the discharge of what they conceived to be their duty."

Sheriff Buchanan was soundly defeated by the Klan-supported candidate in his next reelection bid. But a candidate for county attorney who ran on a platform of prosecuting the sheriff for murder won, although he never carried out his campaign promise.

Realizing that his political career was ruined, Buchanan later opened a service station/grocery store on Waco's east side.

The ire of the community over the Lorena incident reflected the mood behind the fast-growing Klan, which had little connection with its post-Civil War predecessor. The new Klan was spawned in Georgia just before World War I by an ex-minister and promoter, Colonel William J. Simmons. When America entered the war, early Klan leaders seized the opportunity to "protect the nation against alien enemies, slackers, and immoral people." White-robed members of the secret fraternity broke up labor strikes, hunted draft dodgers, and silently marched in patriotic parades to the cheers of onlookers.

Entrance into the Klan depended upon one thing: that a person answer "Yes" to the question, "Are you a native-born, white gentile American citizen?"

After the war Simmons was joined by two other opportunists, Edward Clarke and Bessie Tyler. By 1919 there were several thousand members whose dues benefitted the hierarchy.

Power for their racial defamations was fueled by a postwar recession, which began taking hold as a wave of predominantly Catholic, Slavic, and Mediterranean immigrants hit

America. If a man's business was not doing well, it was because of his Jewish competitor, who was in league with New York bankers.

Klansmen who were taking the law into their own hands had pledged, in their initiation ceremony, to present their bodies as "a living sacrifice to God" and had been exhorted by the Kludd, or Klan chaplain, to "be transformed by the renewing of your mind that you may prove what is good and acceptable in the perfect will of God."

Hanging, tarring and feathering, and merciless beatings—the perfect will of God! Men who believed this must certainly be insane, I thought. But those who had first shuddered at the Klan's unrelenting persecution of minority groups later joined it anyway because of the social pressure exerted upon them. Many spokesmen for the Klan were ministers of some of the leading Protestant denominations who were probably spurred on by fears of Papal supremacy.

As the Klan grew, it spread throughout the North and South until, at its peak in 1924, some 4½ million Americans were KKK members. Not only was it strong in the deep South, but it had also become a powerful political force throughout the Midwest and Northwest, sending many congressmen to Washington.

Intoxicated by power, the "Knights of the Invisible Empire," as they called themselves, became vigilantes. In Macon, Georgia, the Klan ordered all Syrians to leave town. In Florida, a Greek was flogged for going out with a "white" woman. In Texas, Klan goon squads were credited with over five-hundred tar-and-feather parties and whippings, including other assaults and homicides.

I saw the results of one of these in Waco.

There had been rumors about the moral character of a local white man. Though nothing had been proven by the authorities, there were some who whispered he was a pimp.

As he was strolling down the sidewalk one day at noon, two automobiles full of hooded men swerved to the curb next to him. The men rushed out, seized the unsuspecting white man, and threw him into the car. With a quick burst of speed, the two cars raced to a wooded park on the city's outskirts. There the man was hauled out and the clothes torn from his body.

Several Klan members held the writhing, screaming man while others covered his naked body with melted tar until he was a hideous-looking monster. Then they plastered the pitiful creature with chicken feathers.

Few of them, I am sure, had any idea of whether or not their victim was guilty. As a mob, they acted as accuser, indicter, judge, jury, and executioner.

At the height of the scene, a police car happened to come on the group. Since the Klansmen were in white robes and hoods, the officers arrested them under the charge of "whitecapping," a Texas statutory offense.

The arrest, of course, was big news. I heard that a brief hearing would be held to determine the bonds of the men, pending trial. As an interested law student, I went downtown to the courthouse to attend the hearing.

It was a hot afternoon, and after pressing my way through the crowd, I entered the cool interior of the courtroom in which the defendants were gathered.

I was shocked.

I had come expecting to find a ragtag bunch of drifters and roughhousers. Even though I knew prominent persons had joined the Klan, I had never realized they participated in most of the Klan's activities. But now, I recognized a number of well-dressed leading citizens standing before the court: businessmen, professional people, civic leaders.

Most familiar to me was a tall, dignified-looking man, a prominent Waco banker whom I saw daily in the office building where I worked after class hours.

As I sat on the courtroom bench staring at these solemn and self-assured looking men, I found it difficult to visualize them as the same hooded terrorists who had chased down their victim only a few days ago.

But something even more incongruent struck me. Most of

these men were churchgoers, with many attending prestigious congregations in Waco. I tried to picture them singing
such hymns as "Lead, Kindly Light" on Sunday, and then
tarring and feathering a man on Wednesday. I was astounded
by the paradox.

But if I was shocked by the men I found in court that day in
Waco, I was even more astonished at what took place after the
hearing.

Since both Waco and McLennan Counties were controlled
by Klan members—including lawyers, judges, and
prosecutors—the lawbreakers were never brought to trial.
The grand jury did not even present an indictment. It was a
living lesson to me of what happens to our rights and liberties
when forces outside the law take over and begin a merciless
rule of terror.

Waco, a city of friendly and law-abiding people, was
known for its many churches and its great denominational
university. But at that time in Waco, not only were members
of the state bar failing in their duty, but public officials,
judges, prosecutors, and others had scorned their oaths of
office and taken the conflicting oath of the Klan.

Only one official, a district judge, refused to join the KKK:
James P. Alexander, a judge of one of the district courts who
also taught a class at Baylor Law School during his noon
recess.

In the tradition of the ancient Greek scholars, James Alexander felt it was his responsibility to pass on the knowledge
he had gained through the years to the young men following
in his footsteps.

He patiently taught me the basics of how to try a lawsuit. A
rapport grew between us, and our teacher-student relationship developed into a deep friendship.

I remember how proud I was when I heard that this tall,
stately man of principle would not join the Klan. Like the
sheriff of McLennan County, he stood as a lone and courageous man to me. I vowed to do everything I could to become
the kind of lawyer he was.

43

One day Judge Alexander and I talked about the Klan and the stand he had taken on it.

"It's the Constitution, Leon," he said, "the foundation of our country. The men who worked so long and so hard to produce such an invincible doctrine were, in my belief, God-inspired. For it is one doctrine that can weather any controversy, any argument put against it by man.

"There will always be those," he added, "who will try to go around it because it doesn't fit their individual goals—even though in their minds their aims are for the good of the state or mankind.

"Take that man who was tarred and feathered. It could well be that he was immoral. But the moment the Klan picked him up outside the law, you, I, and every other citizen was in mortal danger."

He turned and gazed out of our classroom window. "Perhaps someday people may feel that a judge who decides against joining such an organization is an enemy of the country. Perhaps they may decide that anyone with a foreign-sounding name is suspect.

"Against this we have only one defense, next to God, and that is the United States Constitution. God help us, if anyone in authority ever tries to subvert it."

Judge Alexander smiled at me. "It's good to know we have all these aspiring young lawyers anxious to defend it."

Later I was encouraged when other clear-thinking people courageously acted in the face of rising Klan activities.

Forty-nine members of our state legislature petitioned for an antimask law. Civic and business groups such as the American Legion, chambers of commerce, the Texas Bar Association, and others denounced the Klan vociferously. Texas newspapers chastised the group, and people in Dallas banded together in an anti-Klan citizens' league.

In the end a strong citizenry acting in revulsion against Klan brutality helped bring others to their senses. Across the nation enforcement of the law and political action weakened the Klan to where it deteriorated as fast as it had gained strength. Many Klansmen who had been swept into office were voted out, and by the late 1920s, the Klan had faded into near obscurity.

Our country had been saved from the menace of lawlessness and anarchy. In the future other countries would not be so lucky, but I did not know that then.

I did realize that I had chosen a noble profession, which was entrusted with guarding the dreams my father had traveled four thousand miles to obtain: life, liberty, and the pursuit of happiness under his beloved Lord. I returned to my studies renewed, committing myself to the words of Daniel Webster, "The law it has honored us, may we honor it."

5
Innocent
Until Proven Guilty

In 1925 at the age of nineteen I was ready to graduate from Baylor Law School. But now I faced a problem. I could not be admitted to the State Bar of Texas until I was twenty-one, nor could I work on a master's degree until that age. So I went to court and had my disabilities as a minor removed, thus admitting me to the state bar at nineteen.

However, I felt I still needed much experience and education before practicing my profession. The next step, I reasoned, would be to get a master of law degree.

But which school? I remembered my dean at Baylor had his master's from George Washington University in the nation's capital. I admired him and felt I couldn't do much better, so I wrote George Washington U. and waited, meantime continuing as a secretary in local law offices.

One evening after returning from work, mother handed me

an envelope with the George Washington University return address. My heart leaped, but after opening the envelope I was crushed.

George Washington University simply didn't recognize Baylor's five-year-old law school. Baylor University was a highly esteemed, venerable institution, but the fledgling law school had not yet been accredited.

I brooded a bit and then thought: Why not put my education to work and write an appeal? I was an honor student at the law school and had good grades; in fact my last term grades were the highest in the class. I sent these on to the dean of George Washington University and let them speak for me. A telegram came back from the dean telling me to come ahead.

Mother, father, and Mary proudly attended my Baylor graduation on June 19, 1925. The next morning they took me to the same railroad station from which I had emerged as a goggle-eyed little boy eleven years earlier. Now a tall and lanky young man, I was ready to leave home for the first time. To me Washington, D. C., was an awesome mystery.

As my coach *clickety-clacked* across the Texas plains I prayed that I would be given strength to meet the new challenge facing me in our nation's capital two thousand miles east. A day later we reached Saint Louis, where I changed trains, and the following morning I watched through the window as the Washington Monument rose above the tree line. I walked out of Union Station, dazzled by the sight of the white Capitol building dome looming before me.

I felt that I had come to the center of the universe. I tried to get a room in the Central YMCA but they were filled, so I found one in a small hotel.

The city was warm and muggy, unlike the hot, dry atmosphere of Waco and after all the walking I was thirsty. I noticed a drugstore across the street from the hotel, and sat down at the marble soda fountain.

The clerk walked over, polishing the marble top with a cloth as he came. "What'll it be?"

"A Dr. Pepper," I said naming a five-cent drink that was

then becoming popular in Texas.

"Doctor *who*?" he retorted, staring at me.

Realizing just how far from home I was, I said: "Never mind, give me a lemonade."

I immediately signed up for the master of law degree and began my work taking summer courses. It was rugged. George Washington University had acquired quite a reputation as a postgraduate university in law and in its required courses students had to make a grade of not less than a *B*, on a system from *A* to *D*. All of the sixty-four other graduate students were several years older than I, many of them government attorneys.

To pay my way I became a secretary in the office of Tom Connally, who was a congressman from the Central Texas District, which includes Waco. Since I had arranged my classes early in the morning and at night, I was able to work for Congressman Connally during the day in the single building that once housed all of the congressional representatives.

To conserve funds I ate breakfast and dinner day after day in a small basement cafeteria where I had contracted to take all my meals. It was a gloomy place with limited variety and toward the end of the year I vowed never to return to any cafeteria as long as I could afford to eat elsewhere. (However, under my wife's coercion I have broken the rule a few times.)

Living accommodations became a little better when several fellow Texans and I leased the third floor of a small, narrow office building on Vermont Avenue in the downtown area.

Most evenings found me at my desk in my room. I had found an evangelical church in the area, and when the minister heard that my father was a preacher, he asked me to teach Sunday school. On Sunday afternoons I would take an occasional inexpensive outing to capital city landmarks.

One weekend my brother, Joseph, who was taking a special course at Massachusetts Institute of Technology, came to Washington for a visit. I loved this big brother whom I so well remembered taking care of us in those long-ago days in

Geronimo. We had some great times. I would show him Washington sights, and he would take his little brother to dinner in a restaurant.

Over a hearty meal we'd laugh about the old days and his blue eyes would sparkle with memories. As I looked at him I thought how much I admired this brother, who had already earned scholastic honors at Baylor, the University of Texas, and now M.I.T.

When I told him that I had preached a sermon at a little country church near Washington, he smiled. "You know, for a while, Leon, I thought you were going to follow in dad's footsteps."

My short-lived experience as a preacher had started when the minister of the church I attended in Washington approached me one Sunday morning. "Leon, I usually serve a small country church in Maryland, but I can't make it next Sunday. Could you fill in for me?"

I told him I would and that Sunday evening I traveled out to the church. It was a little white frame building, not unlike father's church in Geronimo, and I felt at home in it. After getting over the usual butterflies in my stomach I gave the sermon, which must have pleased the congregation. A few weeks later I was again invited to speak. Flattered by this return request I worked extra hard on the sermon.

However, that Sunday Washington had a heavy snowfall. The capital isn't used to heavy snows and the city was fairly well incapacitated. I wondered about making it to the little church but decided that I'd better try.

I left early and after some delays struggled through the snow up to its door. Light from its simple stained-glass windows fell across the snow, and I could hear strains from the organ. But when I stepped inside, stamping snow from my feet, I found only eight people waiting. For a moment I was taken aback. Just this few? And then I remembered Jesus' words: "Where two or three are gathered together, there I will be also."

A week later my minister said that he had heard comments

from some of the people on how much they had appreciated my coming that night. I was pleased to hear that someone had seemed to have been helped and sent a copy of my sermon to my father. As I wrote his name on the envelope, The Reverend Joseph Jaworski, I thought about his guidance through the years, how he had stressed the importance of spiritual living. My eyes misted as I realized how much of a disciple of Jesus Christ he was, and I hoped I could be as dedicated to our Lord and Savior.

After a year at George Washington University I had earned my master's degree. The dean called me into his office. "Leon," he said, tapping my records with his finger, "tell your dean that from now on he can send me all the Baylor graduates he wants, regardless of that little school's accreditation."

Now I felt ready to go to work and was very happy to get back to my home city, to my parents, brothers, and sister. I hadn't been home long when two law partners, Tom Scott and Joe NcNamara, asked me to join them. I did and soon their stationery read: McNamara, Scott and Jaworski. A year later McNamara moved to north Texas and at age twenty-two I was a partner in Scott and Jaworski.

As was customary in smaller communities, we did not specialize in one aspect of law but engaged in general practice in both civil and criminal fields. I was already doing a considerable amount of trial work, mainly defending those charged with violating the Eighteenth Amendment.

This was prohibition time, and in small settlements near Waco many people were determined to continue cooking corn whiskey and brewing beer despite the law. Raids on these stills by equally determined federal and state officials were frequent, with charges filed in both courts in Waco. But some of these raids and some of the proceedings that followed were not in accord with the constitutional and legal rights of the defendants charged.

I met with some success in defending those accused of violating the amendment and found myself in demand to defend others, especially in the federal court. A typical example was the elderly man who couldn't understand why he was charged with a crime for doing something his father had done before him. After I patiently explained the new law and prepared to defend him, I found myself again thinking of the seeming paradox of a man who considers himself a Christian defending people accused of illegally trafficking in alcohol.

In fact, a friend questioned me about this one day. My answer was that under our system of justice every man or woman is considered innocent until he or she is actually proven guilty in court by competent evidence beyond a reasonable doubt. It is the obligation of the prosecution to produce such proof and if it fails to do so, the defendant stands innocent regardless of the actual facts.

"The offense with which the person is charged makes no difference," I said. "Unfortunately, some people feel that the lawyer who defends the accused in an unpopular cause is an unworthy individual."

"You mean like someone accused of a vicious murder?" he asked.

"Yes," I said. "If a lawyer were reluctant to defend such a person, then the accused would be denied fair representation and our whole judicial process would fall apart."

"But," pressed my friend, "what if you, as a lawyer, knew your defendant was guilty?"

"Under our law, it is not my function to rule on the accused's guilt or innocence. That is the court's responsibility.

"No matter what," I continued, "every person is entitled to his day in court, and it is the prosecutor's job to prove him guilty. . . . Can the court allow public opinion to be the judge of whether or not a person is guilty?"

"Of course not," he answered.

"Well, neither can the defendant's lawyer judge him, even if he knows his client is guilty. Of course," I added, "where a lawyer knows his client is guilty, he must make certain that no perjured testimony is presented."

I showed my friend the lawyer's stated obligation as followed by the courts and embodied in our profession's Code of Ethics. Basically it stresses that "A lawyer should not decline to undertake the defense of a person accused of a crime merely . . . on the basis of the lawyer's personal desires, his public opinion concerning the guilt of the accused, or his repugnance to the crime charged or to the accused."

But no matter how well worded this code is, it can be an awesome responsibility to defend someone accused of a heinous crime.

It happened to me early in my career in the Jordan Scott case.

One sunny morning in Waco, my partner, Tom Scott, and I were dividing cases we had to try in the weeks ahead. Suddenly, our secretary burst into the room to tell us about a murder she had just heard about.

A young farmwife, Mamie Pedigo, had been found first—shot between the eyes—her feet holding the front screen door of the Pedigo house open at a rakish angle. Her husband, Robert Pedigo, was discovered out back by the chopping block, one bullet in his back, another in his head. The three-year-old daughter was wandering around the little farmhouse in a daze.

A young, black tenant farmer on the land across the Santa Fe tracks, Jordan Scott, had been arrested and had signed a confession with his mark. As the police watched, he had dug a Winchester 32-20 rifle out of a field he had plowed under the day after the murder. Robert Pedigo, he said, had refused to let him come on the property to drink at his well and so he had shot him.

The seemingly cold-blooded murder had the community in an uproar.

After the secretary's announcement, Tom looked at me. "Think I'll put on my hat and walk around the block." He always did this whenever anything sensational happened to pick up the street talk.

An hour later he came back. "Feeling's running high," he said worriedly.

Groups of angry men were gathering on street corners and in cafes. Some of the talk was loud and threatening. We looked at each other. Waco had suffered a lynching a few years earlier and we both hoped there wouldn't be another. Even though the Klan had died down, the racial prejudice it had fomented was still very alive.

A grand jury indicted Jordan Scott for the murders. The next day I was summoned to the chambers of Judge Richard Munroe, who presided over the Criminal District Court of McLennan County. The venerable jurist was plain spoken and gruff, but he had a keen sense of justice and unwavering courage.

He had known me since I was a child, and I had already tried a number of cases in his court.

"Jordan Scott cannot read or write, and he has no money to hire a lawyer," he said. "He is entitled to a fair trial, and he must have legal representation."

Judge Munroe looked straight at me: "I have decided to appoint you as his chief counsel and Sam Darden as your assistant."

Sam Darden was an able young lawyer with about my experience. I was glad to have him with me.

I would have to serve without pay and bear any expense as the state made no provision for reimbursement. But this is a basic service the legal profession renders, one essential to our judicial process.

Judge Munroe pointed out that for obvious reasons he must set the case for trial without delay. It would be held in ten days.

Darden and I would have to drop everything else and work day and night. But knowing the tinderbox atmosphere on the streets, I knew a delay would be dangerous. The first thing I did when I got back to my office was to pray. As usual, I did not pray for a particular result in the case. I only asked God for spiritual sustenance and guidance, and that I did not falter in my duties as a man, a lawyer, and a Christian.

Then, even though my co-counsel, Sam Darden, was out of

town, I hurried over to the jail. The jailer, whom I had known since childhood, said he was expecting me. Obviously word of my appointment had spread quickly.

Jordan hunched in his cell as the dim light filtered from the barred window. He looked up at me, "Is you really a lawyer?"

I explained that though I was only twenty-three, I was not inexperienced. For a half hour I stressed again and again the importance of his telling me the absolute truth. I hammered home the disastrous results of a client misleading his lawyer, and assured him that his words would be kept in complete confidence.

"As God is my witness, I didn't do it," Scott cried over and over again, his eyes brimming with tears.

I reminded him of his confession.

"They said I could either confess or they'd turn me over to the mob. They kept talking about a rope and kept their hands on their pistols, threatening me."

He looked up at me with pleading eyes. "I told them if they'd let me go back to my cell and rest I would tell them I killed those people. I'd been shouted at for hours and I was wore out." He said the officers had then written something down and read it back to him. He had signed it with an X.

His confession said that the white man had threatened to kill him if he ever came near the well, that he thought he had better get him first, and that he had sneaked up while the man was cutting wood and shot him. He told the officers that he shot the wife because she was standing in the door and had recognized him.

But now in his cell he implicated a friend known as Rockbottom Miller, who had just been released from prison. He said he and Rockbottom had planned to rob the couple, but he had dropped out because of fear and Rockbottom had gone ahead with the robbery and murder, then left town.

I dug into Jordan Scott's past, interviewed his neighbors and acquaintances. People thought well of him: he went to church regularly and did not drink. He was a hard worker, seemed mild mannered and peaceable. His former employers gave us the finest reports on his behavior and industry. In the meantime we searched for the missing Rockbottom.

Sam Darden and I felt Jordan Scott was innocent, and I determined to defend him with the same commitment I would extend to a wealthy white man. As an officer of the court I knew that the rights of this illiterate man were no different from any other defendant standing before the court.

When we announced that Scott's plea would be "Not guilty," the threats and pressure from the public began. On top of this we would have to attack the testimony of the sheriff, the constable, the special investigator—all men I had known all my life.

Soon the local animosity became so great that I was hounded by crank phone calls and anonymous letters. There were threats on my life if I continued to defend Jordan Scott. One evening I came home to find my father in a chair, wiping his brow. He had just answered his phone in the study to hear ugly, menacing language.

"I'm not upset by the words as much as I feel sorry for those who lack the courage to say who they are," he sighed.

Some people demanded that I haul Scott into court immediately and plead him guilty despite his claim of innocence and his right to a fair trial.

The anger at my defending him spilled over onto my law partner. One morning Tom Scott stamped into the office, his face white with rage. Two clients had threatened to take their business elsewhere if I did not withdraw from the case. Three other callers had warned Tom of economic reprisal. They said there would be a campaign to induce our clients to find other law firms. We were both aghast that so many people misunderstood the law. In essence they were saying that a person involved in a popular cause was entitled to good counsel. But a person they disliked should have no counsel at all.

How could justice be equal under such contradictions?

Some of the sharpest thrusts came from longtime friends; some had been classmates. I was heartsick over their taunts and threats. Even those who stood by me could not understand my continued involvement with this explosive case.

"Look, Leon," a friend argued, "no matter what you think, there comes a time when one must listen to common sense and not be idealistic. Wise up and think about yourself and your family."

The courtroom was jammed the day Jordan Scott's trial finally started. A deputy sheriff had to clear a path for me. As I inched along behind him, I heard a growl: "There goes that --- of a -----."

In the trial, Sam Darden and I did our best to show that Jordan Scott's confession was coerced.

"Did Mr. Duncan (the arresting constable) talk to you that night?" I asked.

Scott said he had.

"What, if anything, did he say to you about shooting you?"

"He said if I didn't tell him I did it he would shoot me, and he pulled his gun out."

Scott went on to say that he had heard the *click click* of the gun's hammer.

Before Scott left the witness stand, I asked, "Did you know what it meant to touch that pencil?" I was referring to Jordan's mark on the confession.

"No, I didn't."

These points were made to establish that the confession was coerced and to support our contention that the confession should be excluded as a matter of law. But Judge Monroe concluded that under then existing law the jury should determine its voluntariness

In his closing arguments, the district attorney called for the death penalty, and pointing to Jordan Scott, shouted, "This colored Negro, this brute, this assassin."

I rose to object on the grounds that his argument was prejudicial and inflammatory—and improperly injected into the case a racial issue.

When all the arguments were over, the jury deliberated less than an hour. They found Jordan Scott guilty and assessed the sentence as death.

The hush in the courtroom was broken suddenly as one spectator began to clap his hands loudly. But he was quickly silenced by a deputy sheriff.

In due time, I filed a motion for a new trial, assigning as grounds the involuntary nature of the confession and the improper jury argument of the district attorney. When the motion was called for argument, I bore down heavily on the district attorney's inflammatory racial reference. After my presentation and the district attorney's reply, Judge Monroe granted a new trial and castigated the district attorney for the impropriety of his argument.

This gave us time to continue our search for Rockbottom Miller.

Much to our satisfaction we finally located him in a distant town. From all indications it looked as if Rockbottom had been in Waco at the time of the killings.

But our elation was short-lived. When we finally got Rockbottom to the examining trial, he had an ironclad alibi. Yes, he had been in Waco—but not until two days after the murders. Moreover, three witnesses testified that he was in another town the night of the killings.

I felt so guilty about his unjust confinement in the Waco jail that I gave him thirty-five dollars of my own money—a princely sum to me at that time—to help make up for his lost time and travel.

Then I confronted Jordan Scott. "Are you going to tell me the truth, or keep leading me up a blind alley?"

Finally he broke down. "Mr. Jaworski, if I tell you the whole truth, will you try to save me from that electric chair?"

I said, "Yes, of course so," by every legal means.

His whole story tumbled out, more involved than the confession. Pedigo, the farmer, had threatened to kill Scott, and he had ambushed Pedigo in blind fear, then shot his wife to avoid detection.

When the case came up for retrial, we attacked the confession as before. But because Scott had finally told us the truth we could not put him on the witness stand to give perjured testimony. The jury returned a verdict of guilty and assessed the death penalty.

But Jordan Scott had the right of appeal as any other defendant. I had also promised to try to save him from the electric chair.

We appealed the conviction and carried the case as far as the courts permitted. In the end the conviction and the sentence were sustained.

I had defended Scott to the best of my ability. Even if I had known of his guilt from the beginning, my responsibilities would have been discharged in exactly the same manner. The prosecution for the state still would have had to discharge its burden—that of proving him guilty beyond a reasonable doubt.

The entire process was a grueling experience for me, but I was sustained by the feeling that I had contributed to the undergirding of our system of justice by protecting the rights of every defendant, even one guilty of a dastardly crime.

Scott went to the chair, the chaplain at his side, saying a prayer. His last words were: "Lord, have mercy on my soul."

The trial had attracted much attention. Despite the criticism of my vigorous defense of Jordan Scott, there were lawyers in Waco and elsewhere who strongly believed in the rule of law and applauded my efforts. As the smoke of the controversy cleared away, more and more people in the community seemed to approve of my conduct in the case.

In the end I believe it was my prayers that brought me through. As usual, I had prayed for strength and courage, and I feel sure the Lord led me through it every step of the way.

But if the trial of Jordan Scott was a wrenching crossroads for me, a tragedy that happened just after I began practicing law in 1926 struck me so deeply I seemed unable to recover.

6
Two Roads in a Wood

The phone call that fall day in 1926 was disconcerting. I took it in my office, glad that it had not reached our house. The call was from my brother Joseph's boss, who headed the Southwest General Electric Company in Dallas. My brother, an engineer with the firm, had not been at work for two days and his boss was worried. He had already called Joe's apartment and the landlady had not heard from him either.

A cold chill came over me.

"I'll be there as soon as possible," I told him. I went home to pack and told my father as little as I could. Even so he became quite upset. "It's not like Joe to stay away from work without letting someone know."

"Don't worry, dad," I tried to reassure him. "I'm sure he's OK. In fact I've been looking forward to a visit with Joe anyway."

As I drove down the highway to Dallas I remembered all the great times Joe and I had had together not long ago. Before moving to Dallas he had been with the power and light company in Waco, and we had spent a lot of time with each other. We drove around town in his car visiting old friends and had had a good time just talking. He loved to light his pipe and reminisce about our childhood days in Geronimo, the schools we attended, and our visits together in Washington, D.C., when I attended the university there.

Only six weeks ago my sister, Mary, had married. Since father performed the service, Joe had given her away. I was the groom's best man, and Jeannette Adam, my sister's best friend, was her maid of honor. It had been a beautiful wedding. And I thought that even then Joseph was serving as a father to his "little sister."

Now as I urged the car north across windswept plains I thought how the tables had been turned since Joe used to take care of us back in those early days before mother had come. I prayed for my brother as I pressed the accelerator close to the floor.

When I arrived in Dallas, I went straight to the police department, which had already been informed about Joe. They had been checking with his friends and acquaintances. I remembered that Joe had been stationed earlier in Grapeland, Texas, and I got in touch with his friends there. I also called a girl he used to date.

Then we got a lead. One of Joe's co-workers at his office had heard him mention that he was going to a lake near Dallas called Bachman's Dam to look for some duck blinds in preparation for an upcoming outing with some friends. He was to let them know when to join him. However, they hadn't heard from Joe.

Fear flooded me. What if something had happened to him alone on that lake? I called father and told him what little we knew. His voice broke and he wanted to come down and help.

"No, dad," I said gently, "the best thing you can do is stay home with mother and pray."

I hung up the phone and began praying myself, pleading that somehow Joe would show up and surprise us. His bright blue eyes would be sparkling and in his usual good humor he'd say, "Hey, what's all the excitement about?"

The next morning I started my search. Some of the Bachman Dam's shoreline was populated, but much of it was wild. I rented a rowboat and poked along the shoreline, searching for something I did not want to find.

It was cold on the water. The sun hid behind a gray overcast and a deep sadness filled me as I explored practically every foot of the lake. I would not accept the possibility that Joseph was dead. Could a serious bout with the flu a short time back have caused him to black out or temporarily lose his memory?

I conferred again and again with the police in Dallas who checked with other police departments in cities around the country. All the while I kept hoping that I was on a futile search, that something had kept Joe out of town and he would return and surprise us.

But it was not to be. After my seventh day of searching Bachman's Dam I wearily returned to my hotel to find a phone call waiting. It was from the police. Someone had found a body in another lake, White Rock, in a wilderness outside Dallas. They had also discovered a capsized rowboat and surmised that the man had fallen out of it and drowned.

"Would you come down to the morgue and see if you can identify the body?" the policeman asked.

I held the phone, silent, trying to collect myself. Finally I was able to say, "Yes, I'll be right down."

To walk into that morgue was the most difficult thing I had yet to do in life. With one fleeting glance I saw the lifeless body of my brother and best friend, a vision that the years have never dimmed.

I was grateful that my partner, Tom Scott, had rushed to Dallas to be with me. Otherwise I would have been alone, because my brother, Hanni, was on call as house doctor of the Waco hospital.

Tom drove us the ninety miles back home in his Model T. It

was a long, sad journey along narrow winding roads and through small hamlets. Tom tried to keep up a running conversation to lift my spirits but I couldn't talk. I leaned my head back against the Leatherette seat cushion and lapsed into a panorama of memories, priceless moments I had shared with my beloved brother.

I remembered the time when I was fourteen and thought I had become one of the greatest baseball pitchers in McLennan County. I had spent fifty cents, all my salary from the department store I worked in, on a copy of *Sporting News*, which described how to master the tantalizing pitches of the major leagues. I practiced them faithfully until I felt I had become an expert.

One Monday afternoon I bragged to Joe about how skillful I was.

"Aw, I'd have no trouble hitting anything you threw at me," he retorted, grinning.

"I'll strike you out anywhere, anytime, anyplace!" I countered.

"You're on," he had laughed, "for a nickel ice-cream cone."

We had faced off in our backyard behind the parsonage and church sanctuary.

I wound up and hurled the ball at Joe.

He swung and missed.

I threw another.

He missed that, too!

Puffed with pride, I came in with the third pitch, right down the middle. Joe met it on the nose—a screaming line drive that soared right through a big church window and into the room where my father and his trustees were holding a meeting.

I dropped my glove, vaulted the back fence, and took off, leaving my brother to face an enraged pastor who was sure that some neighborhood hoodlums were responsible for the act.

Soon father rushed into the backyard. He gasped audibly when he saw my brother, bat in hand.

62

An hour later I slunk home to face the music. It took all that Joe and I could earn in the next few weeks to replace the window.

Later I had decided that I was destined to be a great runner after my promising pitching career had ended in disaster. Brother Hanni was manager of Baylor's track team and specialized in the 880-yard run (half-mile). Joe, who also attended Baylor, didn't participate in sports. Even though he was 4½ years my elder, I felt he'd be easy prey to my challenge: a race once around Baylor's quarter-mile track.

This time we had a Dr. Pepper riding on the outcome.

To my dismay, Joe spurted to a quick lead before we reached the first turn. He seemed to glide effortlessly along ahead of me with each long stride. I had hoped to avoid sprinting until I came off the last turn onto the final straight-away. But I found myself having to run full speed just to stay close.

By the time we reached the end of the backstretch, my pounding chest and rubbery legs screamed for relief. Exhausted, I slowed to a jog while my brother coasted across the finish line some fifty yards in front.

Needless to say, I was humiliated.

"Nidi," Joseph said, putting his arm around my heaving shoulders, "when you grow up you will outrun me."

Joe could have rubbed it in, I thought, as I smiled at the memory. But he had known a razzing was the last thing I needed for my injured pride, and it was not in Joe's character to gloat.

Finally I remembered the day I had watched my brother receive his diploma from Baylor. I was due to enter the school that fall. As Joe marched across the platform, the university president, Dr. Samuel Palmer Brooks, had announced: "Department honors in mathematics, chemistry, and physics."

Then after pausing a moment he had added, "Not one of them is a snap."

Now he was dead, and I was traveling home to face our father. When Tom pulled the Model T up before our home at

627 South Eighth Street, night had fallen. Our shades were drawn, but light peeked around the edges.

Summoning all the courage I could find, I silently prayed for strength and started up the front walk to the porch, the longest and most heartbreaking walk I ever took. The door opened and father stood there, tears streaming down his face.

We fell into each other's arms, and soon my father muttered softly, "Thank God you, at least, are safe."

Mother walked in from the kitchen and broke into tears. Immediately dad went to her, and began trying to console both of us. "It's all right; it's all right. Joseph is with the Lord and we know he is happy."

As usual, dad couldn't help but think of the other person.

"It was God's will," he said quietly, after we dried our eyes. "We must accept it."

But I had a difficult time accepting it. How could ending the life of a good and kind young man like my brother be God's will? For the first time I found myself questioning what I began to think was a too-pat answer.

One morning a few days later I was walking a downtown street to my office when I met a man who put my distress in words. He was an elderly lawyer who had once served as a judge. A highly cultured man well versed in the classics, he, unfortunately, drank too much and punctuated his comments with profanities.

When we met on the street that morning, he took my hand and said earnestly, "I'll be ------, Leon, if I will ever understand why the good Lord lets so many ---- of ------- run around untouched while he takes a fine young man like your brother!"

"I wish I knew," was all I could manage.

During the next weeks the house seemed so quiet. Hannibal was living at the hospital. Mary was married. And it was just father, mother, and me sharing the little house on South Eighth Street.

I buried myself in work at the law office trying to fill the big empty place inside me.

Joe's death brought my brother, Hanni, and me even closer together. There were just two of us now, with Mary married. I often stayed in his apartment at the hospital where he became known as Dr. Joe. He owned a Buick coupe with red wire wheels and a rumble seat, and we spent many hours in it rambling along the roads outside of town, or along the beautiful winding drives of Cameron Park.

Often two good friends joined us, and we drove along singing such popular songs as "Blue Heaven" and "Shine On, Harvest Moon."

Many evenings Hanni and I would walk the prairies outside of town hunting rabbits. It didn't matter if we found any or not; often we'd trudge along silently, just happy to be together.

The days would find me busy in my law practice and I was enjoying every minute of it. Two-and a-half years passed during which I earned my spurs as a trial lawyer through reasonable successes at the courthouse. I loved being in Waco, and, despite the early antagonism against me, even my well-publicized defense of Jordan Scott had in the end done much to enhance my professional stature.

One early summer day in 1929, two brothers, both lawyers and good friends of mine, asked me to come to their office.

"We've a friend from Houston we'd like you to meet. He's a lawyer and an old classmate of ours. Would you come?"

"All right," I said, "I'll stop by after lunch."

When I walked into their office, I was introduced to A. D. Dyess, a tall, bald, handsome man with a pleasant smile. He seemed like a nice person. We chatted for some twenty minutes, and then I returned to my office, wondering why my friends had wanted me to meet him.

Two days later I found out. A letter came from Mr. Dyess asking me to come to Houston to discuss the possibility of joining him in his law practice. He said that he needed the assistance of a young trial lawyer since his work was confined mainly to litigation. He was handling a very heavy docket and would like to pass on some of the cases to someone else. The two brothers who had arranged our meeting felt it was a prime opportunity for me.

"He's an eminently successful trial lawyer, Leon, whose practice takes him all over the state," one said. "You really ought to see him and discuss it."

I wasn't sure that it was right for me, but I did take the train to Houston to see him. We had a long talk in his office, with him asking my opinions on a multitude of subjects between puffs on his cigar. At the end of our visit the older lawyer made me a highly flattering offer for a young lawyer who was not yet twenty-four.

He walked me to his door. "Take all the time you need to decide, Leon," he said, patting my back. "Sure, I'd like you here as soon as possible, but I don't want to pressure you." We shook hands and I slowly walked to the train station.

The long train ride home gave me time to think. I really did not want to leave Waco where I already had a good law practice and was well known. Moreover, it was home to me; active in church and civic organizations I had many friends in the community of all ages, including state judges, court attaches, and other public officials who had known me since childhood. They remembered the debating championships I had won in high school and the honors I had earned at Baylor and George Washington University.

From every viewpoint, career and social, I had a good future ahead of me in Waco.

But Houston? It was a complete enigma to me. I knew only one person in that big city, a young man who had gone there to run a filling station. No matter where I went I'd meet only strangers: at the courthouse, in my law practice, everywhere. It posed so many unknowns.

What were the Houston lawyers like? Were they more sophisticated, more able than those of the relatively small Waco bar? Would I have to compete with courtroom giants who outclassed and outranked me? What about A. D. Dyess himself? I really didn't know much about him.

When I stepped off the train in Waco, everything looked so

familiar and friendly that I felt it would be sheer folly to leave. I crawled into bed that night thinking that my decision to stay would be easily made.

But in the morning I felt as if I were facing the most important crossroads of my life. Something about Houston nagged me. At work I walked into Tom Scott's office and sat down. The law books on his desk shared space with his high-heeled boots, which were propped comfortably on the desk's surface. He was slowly sipping from a steaming cup of coffee. My heart went out to this rugged, clever lawyer who had done so much for me. He had become a dear friend and leaving him would be most difficult.

"What do you think I should do, Tom?" I blurted out.

He retracted his legs from the desk, planted them on the floor, and swiveled his chair to face me. "I can only tell you one thing, Leon. Do what you think is best for *you*." My wise friend knew that there was no one else who could make the decision.

I discussed it with friends at lunch and over dinner that night. No one had anything constructive to offer.

That evening I walked into our living room to find father preparing his sermon. The lamp highlighted the silver in his hair. My eyes misted at the thought of leaving mother and him.

He seemed to have read my thoughts. Closing his Bible, he put down his reading glasses and looked up at me through kind brown eyes. "Leon," he said gently, "I cannot tell you to go, nor can I tell you to stay." He put his hand on my arm. "But whatever decision you make, I will pray for you, knowing that the Lord will guide you."

Later in my room I continued to wrestle with my decision.

What *were* my goals for the future? I had no political ambitions, I felt sure of that. I did know that I desperately wanted to be a good trial lawyer. But why?

I could only think of the older gentleman I had left sitting at his desk in the living room.

He had left Europe in search of freedom. He did not become

an American by happenstance. He sought it. He struggled for it. He inculcated in his children his fervent loyalty and burning love for this country, and he never let us forget our obligation to it for accepting him as a naturalized son.

I had never contemplated how I would try to make a payment on this debt. But I knew now that the only way for me to attempt it would be to become the best possible trial lawyer.

Beyond that I still saw only a murky trail ahead of me. In endeavoring to come to a decision, I began outlining pros and cons in my mind, almost as if preparing a brief. On the side for remaining in Waco I listed security and a reasonable assurance of success, a happy and fruitful life in a friendly city. On the Houston side all I could see was a big unknown. And yet, something beckoned in that unknown, a glimmer of a larger vista of opportunities and new challenges.

In the end it was the faith of the man in our living room that brought me to a decision, the faith that he had instilled in his children, a faith that convinced us that we could meet challenges wherever we went.

It was also this faith that brought me to the foot of the only One whom I knew could help me with my dilemma. I sank to my knees by my bed and opened my soul to God.

Dear Lord, I prayed, *I need your help. No one seems to know what I should do, especially me. I know that you do, so please guide me.*

I went to sleep that night with a peaceful heart, secure in the knowledge that I had gone to the greatest Counselor of all. He would give me the guidance I needed.

His answer came the next day in a clear, unmistakable conviction within me. I *knew* I should go to Houston. Ambition, a characteristic my father sought to instill in all his children, may have influenced me. But I still believe that the Lord induced me to take the fork in the road that led to Houston.

I phoned Mr. Dyess that I would join him the following Labor Day. I would need that much time to wind up matters in Waco.

As Robert Frost would say:
 Two roads diverged in a wood, and I—
 I took the one less traveled by,
 And that has made all the difference.

7
Turning Points

My Model A sputtered and backfired, and for a moment I wondered if I was going to make it to Houston. But then the engine smoothed into a low roar, and I settled comfortably behind the wheel as the sparse rangeland continued to roll past me.

Soon I began to see the city's then two skyscrapers rising from the horizon and knew I was near my destination. A half hour later I was rolling down the cobblestone streets of its suburbs. It was Labor Day, 1929. The Wall Street crash was two months away, and the state's largest city was still a no-nonsense bustling metropolis on its way up. Houston was something of a frontier town sparked by go-getting wildcatters and pioneering oilmen, who had succeeded the old land, and cattle and cotton barons.

I didn't have any worry about being homesick, for if the dynamic Dyess had lived fifty years earlier he would have been driving a herd of longhorns north to Colorado. He eagerly welcomed me and showed me my office. Stacked on the desk was a mound of pending trial cases and I went right to work. By the end of the week I was bushed, and grateful for Sunday.

The sabbath was quiet in Houston, and as I walked its broad streets, I found an evangelical church, the same denomination as my father's. When the friendly pastor discovered I had taught church school, he put me right to work. But church was to be my only outside activity, for every other minute was consumed by my work.

One morning Dyess strode into my office carrying a mound of folders. He explained that they were records of four trial cases he had won, and now the losers were appealing them. This didn't seem to bother Dyess, who was virtually invincible in jury trials. When an opponent appealed, usually citing Dyess for an error in procedure, he willingly took his chances in the trial court.

"I'm sure you can handle these, Leon," he said, placing them on my desk, and then striding back to his office. As I buried myself in the transcripts of the cases I would have to argue before the appellate court, I knew that if I had any plans to drive back to Waco for a weekend visit I'd better forget them for a while.

One of the cases involved a $10,000 judgment Dyess had obtained against a major corporation represented by a prestigious Houston law firm, Fulbright, Crooker & Freeman.

A leading partner, John H. Freeman, had appealed the verdict, and it would soon be heard in the Court of Civil Appeals in Galveston. I would have to go there to argue it, along with another case Dyess had previously won. I have since forgotten the second case, but I'll never forget the first.

It was cool that November morning in Galveston as I sat in the high-back wooden benches of the courtroom. Sunlight streamed through the big windows. I had driven to this coastal city from Houston early in the morning and had walked into the courtroom at 7:30 A.M., even though court wouldn't convene until 9:30 A.M. I wanted the two hours to think and pray, for I knew I'd be up against formidable opposition from these two highly skilled veteran lawyers.

As I did before every trial, I quietly communed with God, asking him for the strength and wisdom to do my best. A Bible scripture came to mind about letting the Holy Spirit guide one's speech when standing before magistrates.

"And when they bring you unto . . . magistrates, and powers, take ye no thought how or what thing ye shall answer, or what ye shall say: For the Holy Spirit shall teach you in the same hour what ye ought to say" (Luke 12:11, 12). I rested in the knowledge that the Lord would guide me now as he always had.

The bustle of people taking their seats in the courtroom made me realize that the hours had passed quickly. I could see that the court proceedings were about to begin. The perspiration moistening my coat wasn't from an overheated courtroom. Despite my prayers I was very apprehensive.

As the bailiff stood and called the docket, two well-dressed older men made their way into the benches behind me and sat down.

I heard one say, "I don't see Dyess anywhere."

Knowing that one of them was probably my adversary, I turned and introduced myself. The speaker was John H. Freeman, a distinguished-looking portly man. He nodded perfunctorily and introduced his silver-haired partner as Colonel Bates, a member of his law firm. As I turned back to face the court I heard Freeman comment in a low voice to Bates, "Dyess must not think much of his lawsuit."

Hot embarrassment flooded me, and I could feel my neck burning. I realized that at age twenty-four I didn't look like much. Any self-confidence that I may have had began to drain quickly. However, as the embarrassment faded, a cold determination came over me.

When Freeman and I stepped forward to face each other, I was able to forget myself and focus on the case before us. Freeman's reputation no longer awed me and I was uninhibited. The three judges hearing the case leaned forward, listening closely as we argued heatedly, striking verbal sparks.

Finally it was over, and Freeman and I formally shook hands. I returned to Houston to anxiously await the verdict. A few weeks later it came in a letter from the court.

We had won.

I was tempted to tell friends how I had taken a high and mighty lawyer down a peg, but I couldn't do it. Moreover, as I thought it over I felt Freeman actually did me a favor with his comment. In overcoming my anger, I was also able to overcome my self-consciousness.

When Freeman later called me to talk about further appealing the case to the Texas Supreme Court, our conversation ended with his offering to pay our client the full amount of the judgment without interest. Our client was pleased and the case settled.

From then on, it seemed I spent more time in the courts of Houston and Galveston than my rented room, which later became a small apartment.

I was still often reminded that I was in a strange city where unlike Waco, few people knew me. One day I visited a doctor for a sore throat, and as he studied the record card his nurse had made, he squinted and said: "Hmmm, Jaworski." He looked up at me and said, "You ever think of changing your name?"

"Why?"

"Well," he commented, "that's a gosh awful name to carry around and live with."

For a moment resentment flared in me, and then looking at the man I couldn't help but smile; after all, he didn't know any better.

His comment made me realize how glad I was that father had never Anglicized our family name as some people did. I was proud of the Jaworski name, proud of my ancestors who bore it, and I looked forward to passing it on to my children, hoping it would continue to merit record.

"I don't mind it," I chuckled. "After all," I added, thinking of my father's comment long ago, "what's in a name?"

It was humorous episodes like this that I enjoyed sharing with Jeannette Adam on my visits home to Waco. I was able to salvage some weekends, and these saw me chugging north in my Model A looking forward to seeing her again. I was hopelessly in love with this slim, beautiful girl who now played the organ in my father's church. When I went home for Christmas in 1930, not all of my gift packages were piled in the backseat of the Model A. I carried a special one in my pocket: a diamond engagement ring. On Christmas night as we sat alone before the tree in her living room I asked Jeannette to marry me. The glow in her brown eyes wasn't just from the tree lights. In them I saw my answer.

Back in Houston a few weeks later I was returning from lunch one day when I met John Freeman. After greetings he asked if I had a minute to talk.

"Sure," I said, wondering what was on his mind. We stepped into the entrance area of a shoe store to get out of the wind, and Freeman came to his point.

"Leon," he said, "are you entirely satisfied where you are?"

"Right well," I said.

"Would you consider making a change?"

I stared into the display window for a moment, surprised by his proposal.

"I don't know, Mr. Freeman. Let me think about it."

"Well, do so, Leon, and let's talk later." He drew his tailored overcoat around him and stepped out into the wind sweeping down Main Street.

Again I found myself at a crossroads.

The next weekend I went home and talked it over with Jeannette, who said this was something she had to leave entirely up to me.

As I drove back to Houston that cold Sunday night in January I weighed the alternatives. The prospects of joining Fulbright, Crooker & Freeman, then a firm of about ten lawyers and already regarded among the legal fraternity as a "comer," excited me.

But why make a change? After a busy year with the energetic Dyess I felt that I had been fully accepted by the Houston judges and the Bar as a trial lawyer who knew his way around the courthouse. The lawsuits that Dyess assigned to me continued to be full of challenges, offering tremendous experience.

A light snow began to dust the highway and I switched on the windshield wiper. On the other hand, I reasoned, joining Fulbright's small but attractive law firm could possibly offer a better future. But what if the new job didn't work out? After all, it would be a new ball game with different associates, clients, and a lot of hard work to get reestablished. Moreover, I had come to really like A. D. Dyess and knew it would be difficult to leave.

As snow began to build on the windshield, I let up on the accelerator to give the vacuum-powered wiper an added boost. The lights of Houston glowed on the horizon, and I finally decided it wouldn't hurt to at least see Freeman. Later that week I stopped in his office, and he surprised me by offering me a job with his firm at a salary much higher than what I was making, an excellent salary for a twenty-five-year-old lawyer. I said I'd let him know.

He walked me to the door. "It's a great opportunity, Leon."

As I slowly walked down Main Street I realized that there was only one thing bothering me about the offer. There were two lawyers in Freeman's firm who had fine family connections, which helped generate business. I also knew that a law firm's success was not only measured by the ability of its lawyers but by the clientele it was able to draw as well. And I had no connections whatever to help build business for it.

The following week I talked with Freeman several times, and he kept pressing me for an answer. Finally when we met on the street one day he asked me to meet his partner, John H. Crooker, Sr. I said I would and he made an appointment.

Crooker was a no-nonsense man who had been a railroad switchman until he started studying law at twenty-one. After Freeman introduced us, Crooker leaned back in his chair, fixed his gaze on me, and almost bellowed, "What the ---- is the matter with you? Any lawyer in Houston would give anything to join our law firm, but you keep ------- around."

For a moment I was taken aback. Then summoning courage, I looked him straight in the eye and explained that I didn't have any connections that would bring new clients to the firm.

"Listen," Crooker barked, "we don't need anyone to bring us business. We need someone to *attend* to it."

I joined the firm on April 1, 1931.

I felt terrible when I broached Mr. Dyess with the news. As I sat in his office telling him what had transpired, he fixed me with steel blue eyes, put down his cigar, and reached across the desk to shake my hand. "I hate to lose you, Leon, but if you feel this is the best move for you, I wish you success."

I wanted to hug this lean pioneer of a lawyer who was responsible for my coming to Houston. The next several weeks I tried as many of the cases on his docket as I could dispose of. He expressed particular appreciation for this and we kept in close touch in the years following.

After taking my new job I got to a telephone as fast as I could and called Jeannette. She was thrilled and was telling me how well she knew I'd do, when I interrupted her.

"Jeannette, there's something more important I want to talk to you about."

"Yes?"

"Let's get married as soon as possible."

We scheduled the wedding for May 23, 1931, in my father's former church in Waco. Now sixty-seven, father had retired from the active ministry. However, he would be at the wedding to help officiate. In fact, the marriage ceremony was presided over by three ministers: my father, the Reverend Wolf, who had succeeded him at the Waco church and then transferred to Fort Worth, and the Reverend Mohr, current pastor of Evangelical Zion's.

My brother, Hanni, took great delight in the wedding and to my surprise gave a party for me the night before. It was an elaborate affair in a Waco hotel; the tables were mounded high with delicious food, and he had invited many of my friends.

We partied until the early morning hours, and Hanni made a big thing about the three ministers officiating. "It's going to take three ministers to tie that knot," he laughed, holding his glass high in a toast, "to make sure it *stays* tied!"

We all laughed.

Finally, Jeannette's brother-in-law and I made our way to our room in the hotel and fell asleep. I awoke to find the sun already high and quickly got out of bed to start preparing for the wedding. Not wishing to disturb my roommate, who was still snoring with great grunts and groans, I quietly climbed into my clothes. Then putting my hand in my coat pocket, I awoke him with a yell.

My wallet containing all my honeymoon money was gone! Frantically we checked all over the room; then I noticed the door was ajar. We looked at each other.

"Who locked the door when we came in here last night?" I asked.

Neither of us had! Obviously someone had entered the room while we slept.

Instead of paying father for his part in the wedding, I ended up borrowing $100.00 from him. With its backseat loaded with our bags, my faithful Model A took Jeannette and me to Monterrey, Mexico, where we checked into the Ansero Hotel, a picturesque resort.

Unfortunately, it was to be our last quiet moment for a long time. We returned to a little apartment we had rented and set up housekeeping. Even though Houston was not severely hit by the depression, my heart went out to the gaunt, hollow-eyed men lining up for the hot soup served by Houston churches and the Salvation Army.

I caught myself wondering how soon I'd join them when I got word that in addition to my own docket of cases I was to assist the formidable Mr. Crooker, Sr., who was the firm's top trial lawyer. With much prayer and care I helped as best I could and eventually began handling some of the firm's major litigation on my own.

Driving around residential sections of the city one Sunday afternoon, we passed a little brick bungalow. Jeannette spotted a For Sale sign on the front lawn and pleaded with me to stop. Buying a new house was the farthest thing from my mind, but soon I yielded to her fervent pleas to "just look at it."

After a tour, Jeannette was in love with it. The price was $7,000. There was no way I could resist teary eyes and impelling words. I then realized that the resort to advocacy was not confined to just one member of the household!

Once the down payment was met, there was little money left to buy furniture so we bought everything on credit at local stores. Every payday we had to disburse most of my salary in payment.

Soon we both had other concerns. Jeannette was pregnant, and we were awfully glad to have the extra bedroom. Our Joan was born in late June, 1932.

Fifteen months later when Joan was a beautiful blonde toddler, our second baby was due. However, I had an important case to try in Corpus Christi at the time. Was it right that I leave Jeannette?

I checked with her doctor.

"Go on to Corpus Christi," he urged. "The baby won't arrive for a while."

Something within, however, told me otherwise, so I questioned him further.

"What are you going to do," he retorted, "quit working and sit around until the baby comes?"

Accepting his assurance, I left for Corpus Christi. That night I was awakened by my hotel-room phone. It was Mr. Crooker's wife, telling me that Jeannette was about to have the baby. I leaped out of bed filled with fear for Jeannette and anger at her doctor. Quickly I phoned him.

"We don't need you anyway," he laughed. "I'm taking her to the hospital myself."

All I could do was fall to my knees at the side of the bed and pray for Jeannette and the baby. I couldn't sleep all that night suffering the pangs of long-distance fatherhood. As it turned out, Jeannette and our second daughter, Claire, did very well without my presence.

Fifteen months later on December 26, 1934, our son, Joseph, Jr., made his way into the world. This time I was one of the first to greet him.

With my three little children to support, I threw myself into my work even more. Trial work became my passion. It reached the point where I couldn't wait to get to the office to do what I most wanted: trying one case after another.

I'd slip out of the house in the dark of early morning with the babies stirring and Jeannette in her robe seeing me off. I'd race down the block to catch a bus, which would take me downtown. Most often I would return late in the evening, having never seen the sun all day.

But I was doing what I enjoyed.

One afternoon in the office John Freeman asked me to join him in Mr. Crooker's suite. As we walked in together I wondered just what I had done wrong. We approached Mr. Crooker's desk, but he just sat there staring at me impassively.

Suddenly, he stood up, walked around the desk to me, and shook my hand. "Congratulations," he rumbled, "we're making you a partner in the firm."

I was overjoyed, and threw mself into my work even more. Except for attending church, I found time for nothing but the preparation and trial of my cases. Despite the constant pressure, I carried a heavier and heavier load and faced more intense challenges in the courtroom. I felt that it would all eventually determine my stature as a trial lawyer.

Because of my heavy schedule, it was Jeannette who attended the school plays, helped the children with their homework, and advised them on their problems. I had no idea that I would see the children even less in the next several years. But this would not be my doing.

It started one Sunday afternoon early in December when I

was in my study preparing my work for the next day. I reached over to turn on the radio in time to catch an excited announcer speaking these words:

"The Japs have attacked Pearl Harbor and all military activities on Oahu Island. A second air attack is reported on Manila air and naval bases."

Twisting the dial I tried to learn more about the bombing but couldn't. Even so, what I had heard was enough. As I sat there staring out the window into the gray sky I knew this was going to be a war far different from the one I had lived through as a youngster.

The next day President Roosevelt declared the United States at war with Japan. As our country mobilized I began thinking about volunteering for service. There were repeated calls for experienced lawyers, and the Judge Advocate General's Department of the Army reported a need for lawyers to administer military justice.

On one hand I was thirty-six years old with three young children. On the other was a nagging feeling that I should not stay at home when so many others were answering the call. Most impelling was remembering what my country had done for my parents. My father had become a naturalized citizen at the earliest possible date, and no one was any prouder to be an American than he. I was convinced that joining the services would help pay the great debt of gratitude I owed my country.

But there was one person on whom it depended most. That was Jeannette. One spring evening after the children were in bed, I brought up the question as we sat in the living room.

Jeannette was knitting in a chair across from me. When I mentioned the possibility of my joining the service, I saw a frown crease her pale forehead and knew that this was the last thing she wanted to see. But she kept on knitting quietly, then looked up with a strained smile and said, "I know you feel a responsibility. You do what you think is right."

When I looked into the possibilities, I learned that I would receive a commission as a captain. The pay, of course, was modest, but I was fortunate to have some savings plus some small oil and gas royalties I had earned as a partner in the firm. It would be sufficient to sustain my family. I thought about the thousands of other men called to serve who had to leave their families without any security at all except for their allotment pay, and felt very thankful.

Again I found myself going to Washington, D.C. This time it was for an orientation course in the Judge Advocate General's School. I had no idea of what lay ahead of me, but if an angel had whispered in my ear I doubt I would have believed him.

8
A Road to Hell

"Links! Zwei! Drei! Vier!"

Some fifty German soldiers advanced toward me, their leader shouting hoarse cadence as desert boots struck up misty puffs of Arkansas dust.

I studied their faces as they passed, skin bronzed by the Sahara sun where they had served under Field Marshal Rommel. Some were youthful, open; others grim and hard-bitten.

Which ones? I wondered. Which ones were the killers?

One or more of these men marching past me had savagely murdered one of their own. It was my job to find and prosecute the guilty ones. But right now I was baffled and concerned, for we were getting nowhere in what was developing into a serious problem for our government.

Camp Chaffee, Arkansas, was one of the many prisoner-of-war camps in the southwestern states under the jurisdiction of the Eighth Service Command to which I had been assigned. In recent months there had been a number of mysterious killings in these camps. They usually took place at night when the American guards withdrew to outer perimeters. The murders had escalated to a point where the United States was gravely concerned. Under the Geneva Convention, our government was obligated to care for each prisoner's health and safety. Now it looked like we were losing control.

When I entered the service two years ago, I had no idea I would be involved in this kind of investigation. From Texas I had been sent to the Judge Advocate School in Washington, D.C., to learn Army legal procedures. There I would have ended up behind a Pentagon desk if I hadn't asked for a field assignment. Sent to Fort Sam Houston in San Antonio, I had worked with the FBI and other law enforcement agencies to coordinate the arrest and trial of soldiers charged with civil crimes.

One day my commanding colonel, Julien C. Hyer, had called me into his office. "Why didn't you tell me you were a trial lawyer?"

"No one ever asked."

It turned out that he had happened to talk with a mutual lawyer friend from Houston. From then on I served as a trial judge advocate in army court martials, a post similar to a prosecuting attorney in civil courts.

Since the German prisoner murders were in camps under our command with Colonel Hyer as staff judge advocate, they became our responsibility.

Now as I sat at my desk sifting through the evidence, I remembered the first case we had handled. Four men had beaten an innocent fellow prisoner to death. Not only were there two eyewitnesses, but the accused admitted the act. Most of the prisoners were lean. muscular, young men, the pride of Rommel's North Afrika Korps. Many were fanatic Nazis. Their zeal fired in the Hitler Youth Corps, they determined to keep nazism aflame in the American camps.

Just because the victim had expressed disagreement with certain phases of Nazi ideology, he had been savagely beaten and his skull crushed. Each of the accused had pleaded not guilty on the ground that the victim was a traitor and they had been justified in killing him.

I had been dumbfounded at their plea. Their victim had done nothing more traitorous than simply thinking for himself.

For that very reason we had had to be extremely careful in presenting the prosecution's case, even though we had two eyewitnesses to the murder. This had been the first trial of its kind in American history and probably the first ever held under all the provisions of the Geneva Convention in keeping with international law.

A Swiss representative had been asked to attend the trial. Not only did we want him to be fully satisfied with its fairness, but we knew how carefully the German authorities would study the trial record when it was delivered by the Swiss representative. If they had been able to find any flaw in our proceedings, we knew it would be ammunition in their propaganda war against us. Moreover, American flyers were being held in German POW camps and the risk of reprisal troubled us no end.

The defendants had been tried, found guilty, and sentenced to death. The trial records and sentences had been reviewed by our commanding general, the judge advocate general of the United States Army, and the secretary of war. After review and confirmation of the sentences by President Franklin Roosevelt, the defendants had been executed.

I leaned back in my chair and stared out of the window. In the distance the camp flagpole stood in view with our flag snapping and waving against the blue sky.

How many Americans who thought for themselves, no matter how unpopular their views might be, were protected by that flag? I remembered my father's congregation who saw nothing wrong with singing in German during World War I and the lone sheriff of McLennan County who had defied the powerful Ku Klux Klan rally marchers. Now I better understood the news stories on the rapid spread of nazism.

Hitler's demand for *lebensraum* had promised an expanded economy for the German people. Although many recognized the moral wrong of his programs, they had chosen to compromise with righteousness. Thus, individual rights, once greatly treasured, began to lose their meaning, and eventually atrocities undreamed of became commonplace.

I was seeing a microcosm of that same Satanic cycle in our prison camp. Despite the execution of the defendants in this first case, the murders in the prisoner-of-war camps continued and even began to escalate. Only now the killers covered their tracks carefully, making sure there were no witnesses. To establish their guilt, other prisoners had to testify. And this was practically impossible. Fear of deadly reprisal caused any witness to keep silent, even if he was not in sympathy with the crime.

And this is why I had been brought to Camp Chaffee. Whereas in the first trial I had simply fulfilled my duties as prosecutor, I would now be leading an investigation to determine who had committed this latest murder.

Colonel Hyer entered my office and showed me a photograph of the victim. I looked at the thin, sensitive face of a dark-haired youth.

"His name was Heller," said the colonel. "He was only twenty-one."

"Why did they kill him?"

Hyer grimaced. "The kid wanted to send some money home to his bride, and made the mistake of volunteering for work that the Nazi gang felt he shouldn't do.

"It was work he could not be compelled to do under the Geneva Convention," he said. "The gang wanted to make an example of someone who did more than he absolutely had to."

Carefully Colonel Hyer explained what had happened. Heller's assailants had trapped him when he was in his barracks repairing a radio. One prisoner had called in the door, asking if anyone was from Sundheim. He said a man from that town was at the fence between the two compounds, and wanted to speak with someone from home.

Heller, who was from Sundheim, eagerly followed the man into the night. As they neared the fence a gang leaped on Heller, bludgeoning him with clubs.

"He died that night," said Hyer as he placed the photo of the young man on my desk. "I want you to investigate the killing. Identify the ringleaders and bring them to trial."

At first my assignment seemed hopeless. I spent fruitless hours questioning the men in Heller's barracks and poring over the camp records. Who had known Heller's personal history? Someone had used his hometown as bait to trap him.

After relentless probing I was able to isolate several prisoners who seemed to know something about the killing. Though I was sure they were innocent, I felt they were either shielding the guilty out of loyalty or fear of retribution.

Finally, I transferred them to other camps where they would feel safe and might talk freely. Even though I spoke and understood German, I questioned the prisoners through an interpreter. I wanted a third party present to eliminate any claims of mistreatment.

From what I learned, my suspicions centered on two prisoners at Camp Chaffee: Herbert Messer and Emil Ludwig.

Messer had an administrative job in the camp, which included maintaining personal file records on fellow prisoners. Ludwig worked in the camp's infirmary. Both were fanatical Nazis.

From my informants I learned that it was Messer who had masterminded the incident that lured Heller to his death. Messer had arranged to have it done when he was in the barracks giving fellow prisoners a Nazi indoctrination lesson so that he would have an alibi.

I grimaced when one of the prisoners quoted Messer as saying: "The *Heilige Geist* (Holy Ghost) will wait on him!"

Finally I returned to Camp Chaffee confident that I had the information I needed to begin interrogating Messer. It was time to meet this man who seemed so free with godly terms.

The next day I summoned him to my office. He strode in, saluted, and stood at rigid attention, his ice blue eyes fixed on the wall behind me. At age twenty-six, he appeared sharp and cunning. From his records, I knew that he had been an excellent student and youth leader, working with boys in a leadership role in clubs, school, and his church. I knew that in Germany's public schools every German child had between eight and twelve years of daily prayer in school and at least two hours of religious instruction a week before the Nazis came in to power. But then Messer had become a leader in the Hitler Jugend movement, the youth organization that provided the Nazi party with its strongest members.

"So," I said, glancing at his records, "you were a member of the Hitler Youth Corps?"

"*Ja,*" he answered, "a harmless, nonpolitical group. No different from your Boy Scouts," he added with a thin smile.

Time and again I interrogated him, obtaining little incriminating evidence. Each time he maintained his steely composure. Once, in an endeavor to disarm him, I said, "I can't understand how any sensible person can swallow Nazi teachings."

His eyes flashed, face reddened, and he grit his teeth.

For a long moment I stared at him as he slowly regained his composure. Still, I had no evidence on him.

Meanwhile I had a strong hunch Emil Ludwig's part in the killing was to serve Messer as his lookout in the infirmary, where one could learn much of the camp's activities. Yet I had nothing to prove my suspicion.

"Look, you're doing this man Ludwig a terrible injustice in suspecting him," one of my associates said when I voiced my feelings. "He was an ordained minister before entering the service. Besides, the guy is a model prisoner—quiet, polite. He has never given us any trouble."

Finally, I had Ludwig's quarters searched. We discovered a hidden diary, which he had maintained ever since taken as a prisoner.

I read it with searching interest. I wasn't surprised by his derisive description of the United States from what he had seen from the train on the way to Camp Chaffee.

". . . This is America? Poor America. Places like this I had not seen in Germany. All around us we only saw wooden houses, mostly huts, but a fantastic car was always parked in front of them. . . ."

Nor was I bothered by his rancor against his captors. "We were not afraid of anything. They wanted to prohibit us from using the Hitler salute. We succeeded in getting permission to salute in our usual manner.

"Each (American) officer is saluted with raised hand, to his anger and our delight. At the appropriate occasions we sang our national hymns. Each prisoner has the swastika on his uniform. . . ."

But I was shocked by his gloating satisfaction when a fellow prisoner was beaten bloody for failure to adhere to the Nazi line. "They were supposed to be taken care of (killed), but the Americans rescued them in time. But first we really beat them until they were bleeding. . . ."

He went on to detail the victims' suffering and seemed quite pleased that the "defectors" were being punished so well. The more blood and gore, the better he appeared to like it. As I read on, the diary became a filthy thing and I wanted to wash my hands after handling it.

This from a minister of the gospel, a man of God?

I called for his camp records to ascertain if they disclosed the religious denomination he had served as a pastor. They did, and my fear was confirmed. He had been ordained as an evangelical minister and served as pastor of an evangelical church, one of the predominant Protestant denominations in Germany.

The cold, stark fact confronted me. He was a brother pastor of my father's.

As a child I had met a number of evangelical pastors, friends of my father's who served congregations throughout Texas and elsewhere. They were kindly persons who dedicated their lives to God. Ludwig could not be one of them, I assured myself. Not this devoted Nazi who was writing a diary keepsake for his young bride and expressing his satisfaction at the bloody beatings of his dissenting comrades. Was this the same man who must have exhorted his congregations to obey God's commandment to "Love thy neighbor as thyself"?

The murder of Heller was not the act of a soldier meeting the enemy in combat. It was a violent assault on a fellow prisoner whose Nazi ideology was not as fanatical as the assailant's. I had read and heard of the ruthless conduct of the hard-bitten, dyed-in-the-wool Nazi and of his intolerance of those whose beliefs were different from his. But cold-blooded murder was something else. Still anyone who heartily approved of aggravated assault could take the next step and commit murder. Ludwig was indeed a likely prospect.

I decided to confront Ludwig, with his diary close at hand, hidden in my briefcase.

I watched him enter my office, a tall, well-built young man in his late twenties with dark hair. His brown eyes, behind steel-rimmed glasses, evaded mine. For a while we discussed his youth, education, and preparation for the ministry.

"My father is a retired minister," I said.

He seemed interested, and I explained how my father had emigrated to the United States from Germany and told about the congregations he had served in Texas. Ludwig relaxed somewhat as we talked about a minister's work.

"I'm sure you're well acquainted with both its satisfactions and sacrifice," I said.

He nodded. "*Ja*, for a few years I have been a minister."

Then I shifted our conversation to the continuous killings in the camp, finally commenting, "Something must be done about them, don't you agree?"

He nodded, though I noticed him shifting uncomfortably in his chair.

"It must be particularly odious to you, a minister of the gospel," I said, studying him closely.

He sighed, looking at the ceiling. "*Ja*, I am saddened by these terrible things. It hurts me here," he said, pointing to his heart. "But," he added, spreading his palms up in a gesture of helplessness, "what can anyone do about it? It is too late to change my comrades."

I did not answer him. Instead, I reached into my briefcase, removed his diary, and laid it on the table in front of him.

For a long time I fixed my eyes on him. The room was silent. Beads of perspiration grew on his brow and he began to shift uncomfortably.

"What is your explanation?" I asked quietly.

He blinked at me, then stared at the floor. "You just do not understand," he mumbled.

It was the one truth he had spoken. I could not understand how a minister of God could be applauding violence and murder. As I watched him shuffle out of the room I wondered. Was this what nazism was engendering? Twisting godly people into brutal, pragmatic robots? And yet, it could happen anywhere, I had to admit, remembering what prejudice had done to once God-fearing people in my own community.

Unfortunately, I could not find enough legal proof to convict Ludwig so no charges were filed against him. However, his diary was sufficient to transfer him to another camp where instead of a trusted position, he received the bare minimum of rights under the Geneva Convention.

It was a different matter, however, with Messer. I felt sure that he had planned Heller's death. But the problem of convicting him seemed insurmountable. I couldn't find a witness who would do more than implicate him.

Finally, I achieved some rapport with a top-ranking, noncommissioned German officer in the compound where the killing took place.

I liked this man, Sergeant Abar. Though obviously a professional soldier, snapping to attention with a click of his heels when I entered his room, he was not a Nazi fanatic. There was no evidence that he had been involved in the killing, and I sensed he was a man of deep honesty and high principles.

In keeping with this, he wanted to take the entire blame for the crime on himself. "After all, it happened in my camp," he said, offering me a written statement, in which he not only accepted full responsibility, but was prepared to accept whatever punishment followed.

We sat across from each other—I a lawyer, he a professional soldier—both of us dedicated to our callings, which made us enemies. And yet, in a strange way we were friends. For I believe we shared a respect for honor and truth.

As I pushed his written statement back at him, I studied this intelligent-looking man and wondered what would have happened to nazism if more like him had stood up for right at a time when such voices could still be heard in his country. Neither of us, I felt, would be sitting where we were at that moment.

Day after day we sat in that same room through extensive discussions, much persuasion, and argument, until I finally convinced Abar to appear as a witness in court. There he stated that Messer had spoken to him about organizing a goon squad to punish Heller.

Messer received the death sentence, but on review, because the evidence was circumstantial, his sentence was reduced to a long period of confinement at Fort Leavenworth.

When the Nazis in the prisoner camps learned that their crimes would be doggedly investigated, the killings stopped. But I could not forget the men I had prosecuted. How could obviously intelligent men, raised with religious principles, become mindless slaves to an ideology based on hatred and oppression? Even Sergeant Abar, a man I had come to admire as a soldier of honor and integrity. Where was he when the killings took place? By his own admission he knew about them.

In the months to come I was to discover a harrowing insight into this paradox. For there were countless Messers, Ludwigs, and Abars in Nazi Germany. And compared to the prison-camp killings, the crimes committed by them or with their knowledge were horrifying.

But even more shattering was the realization that no nation, no people, no matter how civilized they appeared to be, was beyond falling into the same terrible syndrome.

I saw it happen in our own United States Army in Seattle, Washington. American troops on their way to the Pacific were barracked near a POW camp holding Italian Army prisoners.

One night after much reveling, a large number of American soldiers forced their way into the POW compound where they beat and terrorized the prisoners, including the guards. After the violence, one prisoner was found hanging from a barrack's rafter. It was never established whether he had been murdered or committed suicide in terror. Others were severely cut and beaten.

The secretary of the war was shocked and angered. The United States had the responsibility for the safekeeping of these soldiers. Italy had capitulated. Under the Geneva Convention, we owed these soldiers our protection. The judge advocate general called Major General Richard Donovan to whose command I was assigned and asked that I be made available to investigate the entire affair and to prosecute the soldiers that were involved. The occurrence of this riot at nighttime made the assembling of reliable evidence very difficult, and the identification of some of the culprits could not be definite.

Forty-four accused soldiers were brought to trial in one court-martial hearing. Because of the large number of defendants, a vacant warehouse was converted into a courtroom. Sufficient evidence of identification was not available for some who had been charged, so ultimately the court-martial found twenty-eight of the accused guilty.

All men can break the law, and people of all nations can act without humanity. But what counts in the end is what their fellowmen do about it.

The Bible tells us that the road to hell is smooth and wide. I was soon to see how such a road comes into being.

9
Heil Deutschland!

I slumped on the edge of a creaking iron bed in a Paris hotel at 2:00 A.M., suffering from fatigue and a deep concern for what lay ahead of me. It was January, 1945; an icy wind rattled the window shutters of my blacked-out room. Germany's dying thrust, resulting in the Battle of the Bulge, was being blunted and hopefully the war was in its final stages.

My fatigue stemmed from hunching for too many hours in a propeller-driven Army Air Corps plane, which had groaned its way from Washington, D.C., to Newfoundland, to the Atlantic Azores, and finally to Orly Field in Paris where we had landed a few hours ago.

I was about to step into a sensitive situation where I was not wanted. The judge advocate general in Washington had sent me here to take charge of the prosecution of war crimes trials in the American zone. But General Betts, the European Theater's judge advocate under Eisenhower, wanted nothing to do with me. He was a West Point graduate and wanted a West Point man to handle these trials.

Washington had sent all 132 pounds of its top secret records on war crimes along with me to deliver to him in an attempt to impress General Betts with its confidence in me. But I sensed this would have little effect on the general.

After staggering bleary-eyed off the plane at Orly, I had had to find a U.S. Army vault in which to safely store the records. Then I had dragged myself to this hotel room. Tired and aching, I sat down on the edge of the bed and wished I did not have to see anyone in the morning, particularly General Betts. I reached down, slipped off my shoes, and stared at my olive drab socks.

What was I doing here?

I glanced at my watch. It was 7:00 P.M. back home in Houston. Jeannette would be seeing that the children were in bed. How I missed them all! I leaned against the white plastered wall and wondered if I had done the right thing in requesting this overseas assignment.

Tired, despondent, and worried about tomorrow, I had no one to turn to but my own Counselor. There in that hotel room I asked God to bless my loved ones at home and give me the strength and guidance to fulfill my responsibility in the best interest of everyone. As I rested in my Lord a sense of reassurance filled me and I felt better. After switching off the light, I opened the blackout curtains. The skyline of Paris was etched against a starlit sky, and I knew that no matter what would come, my Lord would be there to sustain me.

I awakened early the next morning with a sense of excitement. I was anxious to get to my headquarters, even though I wasn't sure what my reception would be. As I walked down the sidewalk toward the subway station, people were chattering in French and the streets teemed with bicycles. I felt exuberant. The brilliant sunshine glinted off shop windows, and in the distance the Eiffel Tower soared against a cold winter sky.

But my enthusiasm quickly cooled when I reached General Betts's office.

"What in the ---- does Washington expect of me?" he barked, slamming down the orders I had just presented to him. He expressed disgust at what he felt was a maneuver to slip me into the prosecutor's post over his objections.

Normally, his implication that I was not good enough would have angered me. But for some reason I felt strangely calm. Perhaps it was the assurance I had received from my Lord the previous night.

"General Betts, I don't care what kind of assignment you give me. I'm here to help you.

"Look," I continued, "let's forget about what they want in Washington. I'm not responsible for that. Just give me something to do; I don't care how menial it is."

He glanced at me quickly, then seemed to relax in his chair. Out of the long ago, my father's voice echoed: "Remember, Leon, a soft answer turneth away wrath."

Perhaps it had turned away immediate anger, but it didn't stop General Betts from taking me up on my offer "to do something; I don't care how menial. . . ." He assigned me to an office where as a lieutenant colonel I was outranked by four full colonels and served at a much lower level than the prosecutor's post to which I had been assigned.

However, I relaxed and did what was given me to the best of my ability. Within a short time I was placed in charge of the division responsible for examining the evidence of war crimes. A few weeks later I found myself also in charge of the division investigating the cases. None of this happened because I pressed for it. Again I realized that if we leave things in the hands of God, everything works out for the best.

The other colonels eventually moved on to new capacities except for one, Colonel Clio Straight, who continued to handle administrative work. I had developed a warm friendship with this genial, well-built man, who was nicknamed "Red" because of his red hair. He was knowledgeable in army ways and guided me over many rough spots.

For weeks I dug through notebooks and case histories of war crimes that had been discovered as happening in the American zone. At the same time the British, French, and Russian armies were investigating crimes in their own zones.

If I was surprised by the prison-camp murders in the United States, I was horrified by what had taken place in Nazi Germany. They had openly violated long-recognized rules of land warfare as agreed to by the United States and Germany in the Hague Convention of 1907 and Geneva Convention of 1929.

As bestial as war is, it is governed by written and unwritten laws to avoid unnecessary hardships on both combatants and civilians and to protect prisoners' fundamental human rights. Trials of those violating these laws have been held through the ages, including those conducted by our own government in Revolutionary War days.

If violators went unpunished, such treaties would become meaningless. War, evil as it is, would sink to even deeper depths with no quarter given, and women and children would be slaughtered ruthlessly.

It was evident that Nazi Germany had already reached this depth. Though German soldiers and sailors committed relatively few war crimes, many of the Nazi hierarchy and party members were responsible for some of the most shocking evils in the history of man.

One of these took place in a little town called Rüsselsheim. As I studied the atrocity and learned about the people who had committed it my mind wandered back in time to imagine Rüsselsheim before the Nazi era.

A typical small town in the state of Hesse, its quaint, tile-roofed houses lined neat, well-kept streets that reflected the industry of its people, many of whom worked at the large Opel automotive plant just outside town.

Soaring above the red tile roofs were steeples of Protestant and Catholic churches. In the early 1920s the pastor and priest had smiled and greeted each other as they passed on the street, black robes flying, while ministering to their congregations. Modern shops and offices had composed the business district, and at the edge of town was a peaceful cemetery with stately trees shading a well-kept lawn and neatly trimmed graves.

In my imaginary journey I walked down Rüsselsheim's streets and met some of its people. Coming down the sidewalk before me was blond, blue-eyed Joseph Hartgen, an earnest young man. Reared in a Christian home, he worshiped regularly at his church. He was good to his parents, excelled in schoolwork, and came home every afternoon to bend his blond head over schoolbooks.

Around the corner I met two sisters as they opened their little tobacco shop, which they had operated for years. They worked in it every day except Sunday when they hurried down the cobblestone street to take communion at their church.

Sitting together on a bench under a linden tree were two middle-aged men, Herr Sliker and Herr Junter; as they discussed the events of the day, one of them commented on a former paperhanger and artist who was endeavoring to start a new political party and they laughed uproariously at his being such an upstart.

My mind then traveled about four thousand miles west where at this same moment eight young American men were yawning, stretching, and preparing to get out of bed to begin their day. Some got ready to go to school; others put on work clothes.

Years pass. War is declared between our two countries. The young Americans say good-bye to parents, wives, and children, and they all join the flight crews of Army Air Corps bombers. They take part in missions over Europe. Meanwhile other Allied planes bomb the Opel works near Rüsselsheim.

And now my imagination becomes cold reality as I read the record of what happened to these young Americans in Rüsselsheim. Each of their planes is at some time caught by enemy fire and crashes. Each of them survives the crash and is captured by German troops. Finally they are transferred to a

POW camp for captured airmen near Frankfurt via a prison train. To reach Frankfurt, the train must pass through Rüsselsheim. However, the tracks that pass by the Opel works have been cut by bombing and the train grinds to a halt outside Rüsselsheim.

The Americans are ordered out of their prison car; stretching and breathing deep of the fresh air, they are grateful for the exercise. After they are arranged in close formation, two German soldiers begin walking them through town toward the opposite end, where they'll board another train to continue their journey.

As their boots scrape the cobblestones heads pop from doorways and exclamations are heard.

"*Amerikanische!*"

"*Piloten!*"

Soon a small group of townsfolk walk along with the airmen, staring at them bitterly. A low murmur begins and it builds; a strident order is shouted, "Get them! Kill them!"

It is Herr Hartgen, the blond young man of my reverie, now middle-aged, a Nazi zealot, and the town's propaganda leader. His blue eyes flame with hate as he picks up a rock and hurls it at one of the airmen.

For a moment, the crowd hesitates; then a few also pick up rocks and throw them at the Americans. The two sisters who run the tobacco shop begin screaming hoarsely, "Beat them! Beat them to death!"

Others pick up the chant and suddenly the townspeople become an enraged mob and converge on the prisoners. The German soldiers are pushed aside and become powerless. Two sixty-year-old men, whom I had imagined meeting in the park, begin beating the airmen with clubs, both panting from the exercise to which they are unaccustomed. As they swing heavy sticks at the men's faces, another man raises a spade high and slams it down on the head of one of the fliers.

A house on the street is being reroofed and a pile of tiles is at the curbing. People pick up these handy weapons and hurl them at the men. One townsman chooses a broken tile and drives it point first into the skull of one of the Americans.

A madness seems to thrill the attackers. The voices of the sisters rise shrilly as they urge others to join in the beatings. The airmen are cursed, spat upon, and kicked but try to continue marching. They try to protect each other, raising arms, ducking rocks, trying to shield others from the blows. One man slumps to the ground and lies motionless, blood pouring from his head. A fellow flier hoists him on his back and staggers on.

The flailing clubs and flying rocks subside as the crowd seems to catch its breath. But Herr Hartgen will not have it; he begins whipping them back into a frenzy while screaming for other townsfolk to join in the beatings.

A couple of the airmen crumple to the ground under the renewed blows. Their heads are battered in. The rest of the men pass in front of the Protestant church. Inside, the minister is meeting with some of his congregation. A member rushes in to announce what's happening outside. The minister starts in his chair, his hands clenching the armrests.

What should I do? he wonders. And then, *It is not my task. It is the responsibility of the people guarding these men to step in for their safety. Or the task of our local police.*

At the same time the Catholic priest is at work in his study. Some parishioners knock on his door to tell him that several Americans are being killed in the street. He rises, gathers his cassock about him, and starts to get the sacraments. Surely, he reasons, these men will need the last rites. But then, he hesitates and slowly puts the sacraments away. It would be too dangerous to venture out. Under present conditions in Germany, men of God are without influence.

As the remaining airmen stagger down the street, more townsfolk join the orgy, hurling stones, beating, and kicking the men. One flier raises to his knees crying, begging that his life be spared for the sake of his wife and two children.

A farmer, whose own children wait for him at home, glares at the pleading airman and kicks him backward. Another American crumples and lies still, a piece of tile protruding from his skull. One of the older townsmen rushes up and kicks the bloodied head repeatedly until the insides ooze out.

A few remaining Americans struggle to a wall in front of the tracks where they were to board the other train. A small, quiet man is coming home from the Opel Works for supper. Seeing the airmen, he climbs to the top of the wall, kneels, and slams his hammer down again and again on the fliers.

Finally, two hours later, all of the airmen lie still in pools of blood, most of them now shapeless masses of blood and fragments of bone.

The eight bodies are thrown onto a farm pushcart. Herr Hartgen, the local Nazi leader, in a final gesture of authority, pulls his pistol from a belt holster and fires it into the crumpled bodies several times. Then the cart is rolled to the neat, well-maintained cemetery. But a sudden air raid keeps the caretaker from burying the bodies until the next morning when he digs a large hole in a remote corner and slides the bodies into it.*

As I finished reading the many eyewitness reports of the murders, I was sickened. What could change seemingly God-fearing, well-meaning humans into vicious beasts? I did know that as our air force increased its missions over Germany, part of Goebbels's propaganda was to intimidate our fliers with threats of violence on capture. We knew that the German police were officially instructed not to interfere with civilians who attacked our airmen. But this?

As I thought of Joseph Hartgen, the two sisters, and the other "good-hearted" townspeople of Rüsselsheim, I realized that none of us know what we are capable of doing until we reach such a point. As we cannot envision the heights we can reach by placing ourselves in the hands of God, neither can we imagine the depths to which we can sink without him.

---

* It was later learned by Allied authorities that two of these airmen survived. They had been at the bottom of the heap of bodies in the pushcart and had therefore been protected from Herr Hartgen's bullets. In the darkness, after the air raid, they were able to escape into the night.

My mind was still dwelling on this when several of us left headquarters just before dawn on Easter Sunday and hurried through the quiet streets toward the Eiffel Tower where a sunrise service would be held. The air was crisp and our breath made steaming clouds. Despite the tragic scenes in which I had been immersed, my heart responded to a sense of hope in the air. The further we walked, the more khaki uniformed men and women were walking with us. The scene was quiet, broken only by the thudding of countless GI boots as everyone seemed to be immersed in his or her own thoughts. Then from a side street we stepped out onto the esplanade surrounding the Eiffel Tower, which loomed against the dawning sky.

As I looked around us I was amazed. As far as I could see in every direction, American servicemen and women stood in line waiting for the services to begin.

"We understand that there are over ten thousand of us here," whispered Red Straight. "They came from all around Paris to be here."

We stood together worshiping the risen Christ, and the stain of cruelty and stench of death in which I had been immersed seemed to be washed from me—as if I were again being told, "Have no fear. He is risen."

The sun brightened the sky, and I rejoiced in the assurance that Christ was on this earth in the hearts of those who wanted to do his will. No matter how much evil seemed to rule the universe, it would always be overcome by the power of the One whose life we were celebrating this Easter Sunday.

In a short time Red Straight and I were viewing another celebration in Paris. It was May 8, V-E Day. As we strolled along the Champs-Elysees with all of Paris seeming gone wild with joy I knew that it would not be long before we would begin our war crimes trials.

Later that month I received orders to serve as prosecutor of the first war crimes trial of World War II. We were to bring to justice the persons responsible for the death march of the American fliers in Rüsselsheim.

War crimes trials held in the American Zone of Occupation preceded the well-known Nuremberg Trials of high Nazi leaders, which were held later in November of 1945. Conducted jointly by the United States, England, France, and Russia, the Nuremberg Trials represented a composite of all four powers' legal procedure. However our trial would be the first under the Geneva Convention of 1929 and would be governed by the same rules as our army's court-martial trials.

Our staff had moved into Germany with headquarters at Wiesbaden. Now executive officer of the war crimes trial section, I began preparing for the trial. Again I was given an insight into what the dark forces of the world can do to human nature.

We focused our attention first on Joseph Hartgen, the Nazi leader who oversaw the murders of the airmen. However, he had disappeared underground. Finally, our investigation team ferreted him out, and he was rushed by plane to Wiesbaden where we met for the first time.

He strode arrogantly into the interrogation room, his steel blue eyes flashing angrily. The stocky man upbraided me for bringing him to Wiesbaden, and with a rising voice asserted that he deserved better treatment than to be placed in jail.

In answer, I handed him the first of ten lengthy statements from his fellow citizens who had witnessed the savagery that terrible night in Rüsselsheim. After reading it, he threw the paper down on the table in disgust. "Undoubtedly written by a political enemy!" he sneered. "You are stupid to rely on such garbage as proof."

I handed him a second statement and again he castigated the witness. I gave him a third and still he remained adamant. And so it went until he had read seven statements; then he subsided into complete silence.

I left him at noon, grim and shaken. Before leaving the jail, I had his room searched for anything with which he might commit suicide. Then I gave him paper and pencil, suggesting that he write his own version of what had happened to the American soldiers.

"I'll be back at three o'clock," I said, hoping that he would make some kind of admission.

After returning to my headquarters, I began a round of conferences on other war crimes. At two o'clock, in the midst of one of these meetings, I felt a strong urging: *Get back to Hartgen!*

Breaking off in the middle of the session, I rushed to the Wiesbaden jail where we found Hartgen lying semiconscious on the floor in a pool of blood. He had hooked his wrists onto the sharp edges of the steel springs under his mattress and by jerking his arms back and forth managed to slash his wrists.

Beside him was one of the sheets of paper I had given him. Across its blood-spattered surface was scrawled: *Heil Deutschland!* I will reveal nothing.

We rushed him to a hospital where he recovered, and within a few days he was back in jail. Soon he, the two sisters who had done so much to incite the mob, plus eight other German citizens against whom we felt we had sufficient evidence, were brought to trial.

The court proceeding began on July 25, 1945, at Darmstadt before a military commission of six members presided over by Brigadier General Davison. Darmstadt, a larger city a few miles south of Rüsselsheim, had more courtroom space. We wanted to allow as many Germans as possible to view the trial so they could judge its fairness for themselves.

The defense counsel not only included American officers of equal rank with those of the prosecution but also consisted of German civilian counsel, chosen by the accused. These included several outstanding members of the German bar, among them Heinrich von Bentrano, later foreign minister for Western Germany.

The day the trial began, German citizens packed the courtroom to capacity. It as a history-making proceeding, and every morning before court and every evening following it, I prayed for guidance so that justice would be carried out.

Twenty-eight witnesses testified against the accused. Many of them took the stand reluctantly as it meant that neighbor had to testify against neighbor. Others were forthright in their testimony.

In arguing on the behalf of the accused, the German defense counsel said, "You cannot judge these people according to the measurements of the American people, the citizens of the most liberal republic of the world, which has educated its people through the years according to liberty and humanity. You have in front of you people who were excluded from every spiritual connection with the entire world and who were subjected to propaganda, which inflamed the darkest instincts in the human being. It awakened nothing but hatred."

The minister in the Rüsselsheim church who had said that he couldn't stop the murders because it was not his task was one of those who testified at the trial. He was hard pressed to say something good about the defendants. At best, he had not "heard anything bad against them."

But what struck me most about the minister's statement was that although some of the accused had been active members of his congregation at one time, it had been so long since any of them were in church that he had been unable to say when he last saw them at services.

Substantiating this statement was the priest of Rüsselsheim who pointed out that during the days of the Nazi regime, parents were pressured to keep their children away from religious instruction classes.

When the trial ended after seven days, the German civilian defense counsel paid tribute to its fairness. Another counsel member added, "During the last twelve years the German people have not experienced anything like it."

Of the eleven defendants, ten were found guilty. The other was acquitted as only one witness testified against him; thus the prosecution admitted that there was some uncertainty as to the evidence.

Joseph Hartgen, the two sisters, the little man with the hammer, the farmer who kicked the airman pleading for the sake of his children, and two others received the death penalty. The remaining three received sentences from fifteen to twenty-five years at hard labor. When the seven heard the death sentence pronounced, all asked to receive Holy Communion.

All sentences and the trial itself were reviewed by the commanding general of the Seventh Army and then by the commanding general of the European Theater. The death sentences were upheld except for the two sisters whose sentences were reduced to thirty years.

Long after the trial was over, I couldn't help but wonder, would the American people have reacted any differently under similar circumstances?

I like to think that they would. Yet we must remember that the murderers of Rüsselsheim had been raised in Christian homes, had worshiped God earlier in their lives, and had been good, law-abiding people. How much exposure to nazism, the Ku Klux Klan, or to any other group that feeds on hatred and prejudice does it take to transform fine and honorable people into beasts? I do not know.

Of one thing I am sure. Somewhere along the way the murderers of Rüsselsheim had stopped going to church, had, I believe, lost their relationship with God.

Might the same thing happen to any of us? Without a continuing and vital relationship with our Lord, we become a spiritual vacuum. And evil loves a spiritual vacuum.

Joseph Hartgen, one-time churchgoer and later Nazi propaganda leader who incited the murders for the glory of his führer, paid the supreme penalty in November of 1945. I was told that he died with a passage from the Scriptures on his lips.

Our family after my mother died: Joseph, my father, Hannibal, Mary, and myself

The pastor's kids: me (center) and my older brother, Joseph (to my right), my brother, Hanni, and my sister, Mary.

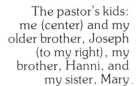

My high school debating partner, Oscar Dodson, now a retired United States admiral (on the right), and I.

Jeannette Adam
and I the day we
were married,
May 23, 1931.

My father and mother when he retired as
a minister.

A photograph taken after I received my
commission as a captain in the army.

Jeannette and our children— Joanie, Claire, and Joe— during the time I was in military service.

The first war crimes trial held during World War II. I am asking a witness to identify Joseph Hartgen, a ringleader of the mob that killed our American airmen at Russelsheim.

A witness reads from the infamous Hadamar Institution record book, a meticulous list of the infants, children, and adults killed there.

My assistant, Captain William Vance, and I listen to the court announce the sentences in the Hadamar Institution trial.

Jeannette and I during the time I served as president of the American Bar Association.

November 1, 1973. I am fielding questions at a Houston press conference after acting United States Attorney General Robert Bork had announced my appointment as special Watergate prosecutor.

My good friend Judge Byron Skelton of the United States Court of Claims swears me in as special Watergate prosecutor on November 5, 1973.

I leave the White House on December 10, 1973. Tapes received during that visit included Richard Nixon's conversations of March 21, 1973, the first tapes that convinced me of the president's complicity.

My grandson, Michael Moncrief, when he graduated from high school.

Our grandsons—
Mike, David,
Robert, John, and
Joe—enjoy
swimming in the
pool at the Circle
J ranch.

The graduation picture of
David Eli Draper.

A recent photo of
Jeannette and me.

10
For the Good of the State

A chill ran through me as my eyes traveled up the tan brick walls of the three-story building from which empty windows gaped like eye sockets in a skull. It was a building haunted by the cries of the innocent, from little children to the elderly, murdered here by the hundreds.

I was in the town of Hadamar, again an attractive, small German town with churches, schools, and well-kept homes. I was standing before the Hadamar Institution, once a sanitarium where people with mental diseases found refuge for treatment.

As a fall wind rustled the seared weeds growing high before the broken, wooden board fence, I shuddered and recalled this building's terrible history. It again reflected what can happen to a society that ignores God's laws and bends justice to its own needs for "the good of the state."

As early as 1941, the Third Reich took a closer look at the

incurably mentally ill and decided that it was economically unsound for the nation to continue feeding and sheltering them. Thus they began the practice of euthanasia, in which these hapless souls were "mercifully" put to death. The local people of Hadamar, caught up in their own struggle to exist in a nation at war, were aware of this practice but accepted it for "the good of the whole." Even they didn't suspect that within a few years the Hadamar Institution was to become one of the most cold-blooded murder mills in history.

As the war escalated and the Reich swelled with Polish and Russian slave laborers, the sickly and starved who were no longer able to perform hard labor were sent to Hadamar for disposal. After all, its staff had proven itself efficient at this type of thing.

In time, those in charge of shunting the useless to Hadamar became less selective. Men and women with minor ailments, and many with none at all, found themselves entering its gates.

From the evidence I had read in my two months' study of Hadamar after my work in Rüsselsheim, I saw them trudging into the doorway of this building, as many as seventy at a time. Weary from their long journey, many limping or coughing, their hearts must have lifted as they were promised beds and treatment.

They were led to hospital cots. Shortly after, Hadamar staff personnel in white coats walked among them, giving them hypodermic injections or handing them pills. They were told that the medication was for the treatment of disease.

All of them died immediately. Their bodies were hauled to the building's cellar, lumped together, and buried in a common grave. All of this was done quietly, efficiently, continuously.

Children whose parents were slave laborers were put to death alongside their mothers and fathers. All who entered the "sanitarium" met sudden death—young, old, sick, hearty, Catholic, Protestant. There were no holidays at Hadamar. On Christmas Day, 1944, two little children were given deadly injections along with their mother.

This continued from July, 1944, to April, 1945. Though we had concrete evidence of some four hundred deaths, we knew there were many more.

I walked through the gloomy halls of the deserted building that fall day. The rooms with their empty iron cots were cold and bleak. Shadows lengthened in the halls and the wind wailed through paneless windows. I shuddered and turned to leave.

I had seen enough.

The trial of which I was trial judge advocate began October 8, 1945, under the United States Army's war crimes branch. The defendants were the Hadamar Institution's administrator, Alfons Klein, head physician Adolf Wahlmann, two male nurses Heinrich Ruoff and Karl Wilig, chief female nurse Irmgard Huber, record keeper Adolf Merkle, and gravedigger Philipp Blum.

All admitted their involvement. In fact, when the slave laborers first began arriving at Hadamar, they assumed that all were to be exterminated since they had limited facilities for the treatment of the ill.

Later, in defense, they said that if they had failed to participate in the killings they would have been punished. However, Alfons Klein admitted that "nobody was threatened with the concentration camp, nobody was told not to talk, and everyone worked there voluntarily and was able to resign at any time."

"Did it affect your feelings or emotions or your conscience to watch these injections?" he was asked.

"It was not a very nice thing for a man to see those people die."

"But you felt also that it was wrong, did you not?"

"Yes."

When Dr. Wahlmann was asked if it ever occurred to him that those being killed were afraid of death, he answered, "Yes, but my death comes closer to me."

Irmgard Huber admitted that she and her cohorts had assumed Germany would win the war; otherwise she had known they would be in serious difficulty for what they had done.

As was true with other war crimes trials, the accused were defended by competent American army lawyers and by distinguished civilian counsel of the German bar. Typical of the latter was Dr. Kurt Kaufmann, who said in his defense argument, "There are two different worlds. You are fortunate to belong to a continent which still remains a democracy. We are citizens of an old continent with an ancient culture under which we suffer."

In the main, however, the defense counsel based its argument on a plea for mercy.

In closing he expressed gratitude on behalf of himself and his colleagues "for the impartial manner in which this court has been held."

The tribunal found each of the accused guilty. Klein, the administrator, and Ruoff and Wilig, the two male nurses, were sentenced to death. Dr. Wahlmann, because of his advanced years and poor health at the trial, was sentenced for life. Merkle, the record keeper, was given thirty-five years; Blum, the body disposer, thirty years; and Irmgard Huber, the nurse, twenty-five years. All sentences were upheld on review.

The day after the sentences were passed, the wives of Klein, Ruoff, and Wilig asked that their husbands be allowed to receive the Sacrament of the Lord's Supper. I'll never forget the exclamation of the jail keeper's wife (who with her husband had never joined the Nazi party) when this request was made.

"Isn't it strange how terrible sinners suddenly want to become religious again?"

Though they had asked for something denied their victims, I was relieved to hear that these men were turning to God and the beliefs they had scorned so long. Again, I found myself pondering the paradox of people who had adhered to God's commandments in earlier years, only to set aside their moral convictions and regard for human life when they were subjected to a regime of evil.

Alfons Klein had come from a good home. Regarded as a fine and bright boy, he had shown much promise as he approached manhood. However, he had become obsessed with Nazi ideology and became a weakling, ready to do anything to please his Party masters.

Dr. Wahlmann had been well educated in leading medical schools and had been a credit to his profession. What made him become a tool of the Nazis? Fear? A desire for approval?

Ruoff and Wilig had been raised in Christian homes. Family men who had lived quiet and peaceful lives, they had at one time been active in their churches. What had made them stop? An inability to face God and continue their evil work?

Their unsavory occupations had not interfered with their family life. Each day they had breakfasted with their wives and children, then went to work to kill human beings. They had returned for the noon meal with their family, gone back to Hadamar, and then rejoined their loved ones for the evening meal followed by quiet repose. How were they able to insulate their act of giving a child a deadly injection and watching his knees draw up in convulsive death throes when kissing their own child good night and perhaps even hearing his prayers? If Ruoff and Wilig were able to do this, how many millions more of us could do it?

Merkle made no pretense of morality. A dedicated Nazi who had joined the party in 1930, he was haughty, insolent, and stated that he saw no wrong in his actions. Perhaps this could be explained by his stupidity. In his meticulous record keeping he, of course, falsified the cause of death of the victims. When a large group of slave laborers arrived, he would be given their names in alphabetical order. But not wanting his records to show them all dying in one day, he would enter a few names at a time so they would appear to have died over a period of time. However, he did this beginning at the top of the list, and thus had his "patients" dying in alphabetical order.

Blum, the burier, typified the spineless follower who never stops to think of the consequences of his acts. His main purpose in life was to go along with the crowd.

By the time nurse Irmgard Huber reached the stand, she evidently realized the depths to which she had sunk for she broke down and cried remorsefully. Witnesses termed her a loving, compassionate person before her employment at Hadamar. What had happened?

Again, I had to admit that "there, but for the grace of God, go I" and other well-intended people if we let our moorings of morality slip. I thought of people crowded in a building who panicked when fire broke out and trampled each other to death in their urge to escape. Could it have been something like this in Nazi Germany, a mass hysteria only in slow motion? I had no answers.

One thing was for certain. The despicable ideology of nazism did not grip Germany overnight. It came as a cancerous growth that by easy stages substituted wrong and evil for right and human dignity. As Edmund Burke warned: "All that is needed for the forces of evil to win is for enough good men to do nothing." And, in fact, there were enough good men and women in Germany who, during the growth of nazism, did nothing. They disapproved of what they saw, but because they remained relatively silent, the wrongs escalated from day to day. Once nazism applied its stranglehold to the free institutions of Germany, the schools were poisoned, the churches silenced, and the courts prostituted. The freedom to protest was annihilated, and the voices of good men and women lastingly stilled.

But I did not feel that this would happen to those who continually acknowledged God's presence in their lives, who truly feared him, and endeavored to live by his commandments. From what I had seen, it was those who left our Lord's side who were susceptible to evil.

By now, with the approach of winter, 1945, I was ready to go home. Even before the Hadamar trial I had accumulated enough service under the army's point system to be discharged. More important was the news from home that my father was very ill.

Day after day for months I had been involved in tragedy and sights of horror, and I wanted it to end as soon as possible. But I had agreed to prepare the Dachau Concentration Camp case for trial, and it was still before me. I had already spent six days watching U.S. Army films on Dachau and other concentration camps, and they had devastated me. Dachau was just one of many camps in which the Jew, the outspoken Christian, the advocate of peace, and other nonconformists were exterminated "for the good of the Third Reich."

When our troops first entered Dachau, the sight was so sickening that many battle-hardened veterans found it difficult not to shoot those in charge of the camp. Now those responsible for the atrocities would be brought to trial, and my last assignment in Europe would be to supervise the investigations for this purpose.

Visiting Dachau and listening to testimonies of what went on there left me numb. When we took it over in April, 1945, some thirty-three thousand people had been squeezed into space planned for eight thousand. Young men, who only a few months earlier were strong in body and mind, had become emaciated and mentally disturbed. Girls in the bloom of life were marked by lines of suffering and abuse. Many were vermin infested and had been deprived of the most basic sanitation necessities. These people had been beaten, tortured, and starved to the point where one hundred persons were dying each day from illness alone, not to mention those being killed outright.

The killings resulted from agonizing experiments on inmates. A man would be placed in a device in which he would suffer sudden, extreme changes of air pressure, usually dying from a hemorrhage or embolism.

A woman would be immersed in ice water for a day and a half to test her physical reaction, which was usually death. Others had to drink salt water for five days in a row to test its effect on them. There were handy gas chambers for the sickly and crematoriums to dispose of the bodies quickly.

But most grueling to the inmate was not knowing which day, which hour, his death would come. "My most terrifying memory," said one man, "was the constant roll calls when we'd stand outside naked in the winter waiting for the doctor to point out a physically infirm person for execution."

At the end of our investigation, forty officers, doctors, and guards were charged with the murders of Dachau. Capable American officers who had assisted in the investigation now took over the prosecution. The trial began November 15, 1945, and lasted nearly a month. All the accused were convicted with thirty-six sentenced to death by hanging. Later, some of the sentences were reduced on review.

Again the appeals for clemency stressed that these men were "good husbands" or "good sons." This was undoubtedly true, for our investigation disclosed that by and large they were all of good character before nazism had influenced them. Again, we found a camp commander who had been a peaceful man with a normal conscience in his pre-Nazi days. The doctors who performed the inhuman experiments were respected members of their profession, and other camp staff members held normal jobs in civilian life.

Yet, like thousands and thousands of others, they had yielded to the Nazi lure, and then, after realizing the full depth of its insidiousness, had lacked the moral strength to disown it. I began to see that the Nazi party would never have attained its great power on the basis of its fanatical followers alone. It had to have help from another source: the countless individuals who did not really believe in Party principles, yet chose to hold membership in the organization and thus passively support it. These included everyone—shopkeepers, mailmen, and prominent leaders. One such leader was Dr. Hans Borchers, who had once served in New York City as consul general for the German Reich.

While still in Germany I received orders from the secretary of war to interview Dr. Borchers. At the time he was confined with a number of other former high Nazi officials in a tiny village in Luxembourg. This was a top-secret location known only by the U.S. Army code name: Ashcan.

A jeep took me past several checkpoints into a beautiful resort town shaded by huge trees and surrounded by rolling countryside.

I met Ashcan's commander at his headquarters, and he escorted me to the building in which the Nazis were confined. It had been a large resort hotel with a wide veranda encircling it. The quiet, peaceful-looking grounds were in contrast to the barbed-wire entanglements. At each corner stood a watch-tower manned by guards armed with machine guns.

It was a steaming, hot summer morning, and as I approached the hotel I was stunned to see practically the whole leadership of the Nazi party sitting casually on the veranda. Missing were Hitler, Himmler, Goebbels, and others who had committed suicide. But seated before me were Joachim von Ribbentrop, reichminister for foreign affairs; Wilhelm Keitel, chief of the high command of the Armed Forces; Alfred Rosenberg, reichminister for occupied eastern territories; Hans Frank, governor general of the occupied Polish territory; Alfred Jodl, chief of operations of the high command; and several others.

Gone were the impressive uniforms. Instead I saw tired-looking, middle-aged and elderly men in rumpled civilian clothing. A few wore undershirts and one was bare-chested. Some were reading, others were writing letters, and some were merely looking into space.

Except for our footsteps on the walk it was quiet as the American officer and I approached. Then he called out, "Atten . . . hut!"

The seedy-looking men on the veranda clambered out of their chairs and stood stiffly at attention. Suddenly, everything within me turned to hate as I faced the men ultimately responsible for the heartrending scenes and cold-blooded murders I had been investigating.

Despite my father's admonishment never to hate one's fellowman—and knowing that God commands us to love our enemies—the emotional surge within me suppressed all else except my anger over what these men had done to their fellow human beings. I walked quickly past them into the building.

I met Hans Borchers in a small bare room. A slight man with thinning gray hair, he, too, wore unpressed slacks and only an undershirt.

He had been a member of the Nazi party since 1936. I had always wondered why supposedly intelligent men like him had supported the party so I asked him this question directly.

He leaned back in his chair and looked reflectively into the distance as if he himself were trying to find the real answer. Finally, he said, "Perhaps . . . if I had foreseen things, I would not have done so."

He looked at me and continued. "Naturally, in 1935, we still hoped that this very extreme attitude would gradually die down, that better elements would come into the Party, and that eventually out of this revolution we would be able to get an evolution." He stopped for a moment and smiled wanly at me. "I thought I could be a helpful part in that machinery."

He looked at the floor. "Most reluctantly I decided to join the Party, although I did not like it and although I particularly objected to the Jewish situation."

In the silence of the room it seemed that I could hear the distant wail of millions of terror-stricken people.

"By the use of the term *Jewish situation*," I asked, "what do you mean?"

He stared straight at me as if he had to say it as quickly as possible. "I mean that the Jews were to be eliminated practically from the German life under the Nazi doctrine, which I thought was unjust."

I sat looking at Dr. Heinrich Franz Johannes Borchers who, like so many wanting to promote themselves in the eyes of those in power, was willing to stultify his conscience and take part in injustice and oppression.

I remembered another well-meaning man who had found himself in the same position. The apostle Peter, fearful and alone, cowered in the courtyard after the Roman soldiers had taken his Lord and Master away. When the maidservant asked if he was a member of the Galilean's group, he had denied it repeatedly until the cock crowed thrice and he realized his sin.

As I looked at Hans Borchers I wondered if he had heard the cock crow.

I left him, sitting by himself in the small shadowy room. There was another former leader I wanted to see—Hermann Wilhelm Göring, commander in chief of the German Air Force and the man who was to succeed Hitler as head of the Third Reich.

When captured, he had been astounded that he was taken to Ashcan along with everyone else. He complained bitterly, stating that he should be accorded pomp and ceremony.

But he was far from pompous the afternoon I saw him. As the American commander showed me to his room he explained that Göring was not feeling well. There had been an electrical storm the previous night—and the vaunted commander in chief of the German Air Force was deathly afraid of lightning.

"So much so," said the officer, "that he seems to have suffered a mild heart attack."

The commander swung open a door, and I stepped into another small dark room. On a bed lay a huge rounded form with its face turned to the wall. He was quiet except for the rise and fall of his bulky chest. My guide nudged me, "You can talk to him. He's awake."

I bent over the corpulent body. "Would you mind talking with me?"

The large head remained facing the wall. Finally, he stirred and in a low, quavering voice said, "I . . . don't feel well today."

"But I have only a few questions," I said gently.

"No," he muttered into the wall, "my heart is hurting me."

I stood for a moment and glanced at the officer with me.

He shrugged. I looked down on the form of the once-mighty man who had vowed that he would conquer the world through his air power. Now he was rendered helpless by the sound of God's lightning. I turned and quietly left the room.

On October 15, 1945, I was aboard a plane taking off from Paris's Orly Field, heading for home. Just before leaving, I had been surprised by General Betts, who had gotten together the whole war crimes staff for an assembly where he had presented me with the Legion of Merit.

I leaned back in my seat and quietly gave thanks to God for answering my prayers that first night in France many months ago. He had sustained me in every way.

The hours droned by; it would be another long flight to the Azores, Newfoundland, and then LaGuardia Field, New York. I was dozing when I felt a tap on my shoulder. It was a chaplain, a colonel. Out of some forty officers on the plane, he and I were the highest ranking men.

I could see he was concerned as he sat down next to me. "We've a problem," he said in a low voice.

It involved one of the passengers, an officer who was rushing home to his critically ill wife. He had gone to the plane's rest room and left his wallet lying on the sink. Later, when he remembered it, he went back to retrieve the wallet but it was minus a $100 bill. He was stricken, since the money was needed to pay his wife's medical expenses.

"What do you suggest we do?" asked the chaplain.

After we discussed it, we came up with an idea. Together, the chaplain and I stood in front of the officers and told them what had happened.

"Now each of us," I said, "including the chaplain and myself, will go back to the rest room one by one. We'll each stay in there for one full minute, allowing one of us to return the bill. There will be an envelope lying on the sink."

There were some muttered exclamations, but one by one all forty of us went back to the rest room in turn. Afterwards, the chaplain and I stepped back into the room and picked up the envelope. In it was the $100 bill.

As the transport continued over the Atlantic and the cabin had subsided into a low murmur of conversation mixed with snores from sleeping men, I thought about how a seed of evil always seems to be within us, waiting for that unguarded moment to take over.

I remembered all of those I had met in the past months who had allowed that seed to grow through callousness, or fear of not belonging, to where it eventually consumed them and their nation.

I looked toward the cabin port to see a flush of dawn brightening the sky and prayed that we were heading not only for a new day but a new world.

11
Secret for a Strong America

My first few months at home early in 1946 were a roller coaster of emotions. I was ecstatic to be back with my family. How I had missed Jeannette and the children. The little ones had changed so much; they were not so little anymore. Claire and Joanie, now thirteen and fourteen, were maturing into young ladies. Joe, now twelve, was growing tall.

We had a large vacant lot next to our home where Joe and I had played football and baseball, sometimes alone, sometimes with his friends. At our first chance we ran to this lot.

As Joe passed the football to me I immediately noticed the difference in his control: more zip, more accuracy. When we played touch football a few days after that, I marveled at his progress. He loved football, and it came as no surprise to me in later years when he made first string tackle on the high school team.

We had just finished running some passing patterns that day in 1946 when Joe called, "By the way, dad, I'm going to be a lawyer, just like you."

I smiled at him. Only a few years ago he had wanted to be a cowboy. Whatever God led him to do in life, I prayed that Joe would never have to undergo anything as harrowing as what I had been exposed to the past few years. The horror of the atrocities, the realization of what man could do to his fellow-man, haunted me like some oppressive spirit, and I asked God again and again to cleanse it from my memory. Why, I found myself wondering, does man insist on creating his own despair when there is sorrow enough in the world?

It was not until some fifteen years later that I could fully reveal the horrible sights and tragedies I had seen and thought about day after day for that unbearable year. It seemed so incredible. And yet I knew it was true. I had seen the evidence, heard the testimony. The imprint of those days remains indelibly printed in my mind—memories that have been reawakened through the years when our country has been threatened by the same ugly signs of tyranny and violence.

Mixed with my joy at being home was another sorrow: the impending loss of a loved one. My father's once strong heart was weakening. The day after I arrived home, I drove to Seguin, Texas, the little town where he and Oma, as our children always called her, now lived. It was near Geronimo; he enjoyed living near the black dirt farmlands where he first began preaching. As I drove through the stark country that was always home to father I was grateful that God had allowed me to see him again.

Even though I knew he was ill, I wasn't prepared to find him so thin, so gray and tired looking. Yet, as always, his spirit had overcome his body; I could see it in the sparkle in his eyes. He clasped my hands in his thin, blue-veined ones, the same hands I so well remembered folded in prayer at our family table.

"I'm so glad to see you, son," he said, his brown eyes

glistening behind his glasses. "You know I've been keeping up on you over there."

We talked and talked. His mind was as keen as ever. We talked about my brother, Hannibal, who had also entered the army and as a colonel became chief of surgery at McCloskey General Hospital in Temple, Texas, then later went to the Philippines where he became head of surgery in the Manila General Hospital. We discussed the old days in Geronimo, and he shut his eyes, a smile on his gaunt face. Soon he was asleep. I looked up at Oma.

"He so looked forward to your coming." She smiled. My heart went out to this lovely woman who had meant so much to us all as a mother and as a wife to father. I thought how second marriages like this one were also made in heaven.

Father and I enjoyed several more visits, and then in March, three months after my return home, he left this earth. He was buried at the little cemetery across the road from the red brick country church where he had served his Lord for so many years. I knew my father would go on to the many mansions Jesus spoke of, and his body would become a real part of the land he had come to love so much. So many times he had said, "We place ourselves in the hands of the Father, and when we do that, what do we have to worry about?"

At this same time I was suffering another kind of emptiness in my work. When I endeavored to pick up the pieces after being gone 3½ years, I found no cases to try, no clients with whom to talk, no challenges. I was miserable. Often I found myself standing at my office window looking over downtown Houston.

What twisted the knife was that the other lawyers in our firm were extremely busy. Legal work had picked up in momentum after the war, and how I envied these men. I found myself longing for the constant pressure under which I had labored before entering the service. Now I found nothing to concern me except the lack of anything to do. I was never more unhappy.

But I should have been more patient. It was as if I was being given a time for readjustment. Before long, my case load began to build, and I found myself fighting the clock again. On top of this I received more and more invitations to speak before civic clubs and other social groups, mostly, of course, because of my involvement in the war crimes trials. I did accept some of the invitations, but each was an incursion into painful memories that I wanted to avoid. It was like retracing one's steps through a dark, miry swamp from which one had just escaped—or from the abyss of hell.

The most welcome of my outside activities, however, was our church life. We had felt led to join the First Presbyterian Church in Houston because of its excellent church-school program for the children. We wanted Joanie, Claire, and Joe to have the best possible instruction in what we felt was the most vital part of their lives. Moreover, I was very impressed by the minister, Dr. Charles King, who had a clear and succinct way of illuminating the truths of the Bible.

The children liked him, too, and church for us became a family affair.

And then I found myself at another crossroads.

It came with the death of James P. Alexander, chief justice of the Supreme Court of Texas. He had been the professor who taught me trial work at Baylor School of Law, and had always stood out in my memory as a hero because of his courageous stand against the Ku Klux Klan. As I remembered this I thought how nazism might have been halted if there had been more men like Judge Alexander in Germany in the 1930s.

I was proud to be one of the pallbearers at his funeral, which was held on a Saturday in March, 1947. Late the following Sunday evening as Jeannette and I were about to retire, the phone rang.

It was the governor of Texas, Beauford Jester.

He said that he and some advisers had been in conference Sunday afternoon and decided that one of the associate justices of the nine-member Texas Supreme Court would be moved up to chief justice to fill the vacancy left by Judge Alexander.

"I am tendering you the post of associate justice and I urge you to accept it," he said. I was astonished. Governor Jester was offering me a post that most lawyers in Texas would give their eyeteeth to have.

"Governor," I said, "this is a real honor, and I thank you from the bottom of my heart. However, I would like to think about it. Can I let you know tomorrow?"

The phone was quiet for a moment. "Well," he said, "call me as soon as you can tomorrow."

I sat on the edge of our bed, my mind racing. Did I want to hold public office? Jeannette knew what I was going through and quietly left me to my thoughts.

In a little while the telephone rang again. I picked it up to hear the familiar voice of John H. Crooker, Sr., one of the two founders of our law firm. "Well, Leon," he said, "what did you tell the governor?"

I was quite surprised that he knew about the phone call. After telling him what I had said to the governor, I asked, "How did you know about it?"

"Well, before the governor talked to you, he called Colonel Bates and told him what he had on his mind." Colonel William B. Bates was then a senior partner in our firm and a close friend of the governor since they had served together in World War I.

Now both Crooker and Bates were anxious to know what I would do. The governor was offering me a prestigious post on the highest court in our state.

Yet, as I pondered the opportunity I realized that if I were to be true to myself, there was no way I could accept it. I remembered years ago when I had felt that God led me to become a trial lawyer; I had vowed to fulfill this calling to the best of my ability.

As yet I felt that I had a long ways to go. That night I crawled into bed with a peaceful mind and had a sound night's sleep. Monday noon I called Governor Jester and explained that there were overriding reasons that impelled me to continue in the practice of law and not hold public office.

He asked if I had any recommendations for the post, and I mentioned some men whom I thought would make good justices.

Almost as if my decision had an effect on cases coming my way, I found myself even busier. After some years passed, I was handling most of the major general litigation for our firm. However, thanks to a number of able young lawyers assisting me, I was able to delegate the details of preparation to them, leaving me to take over the lead as the cases came to trial.

I particularly enjoyed being able to spend more time with my family. Through the years we had made it a tradition to vacation together at guest ranches where all of us loved horseback riding, fishing in lakes and streams, and eating chuck-wagon chow. Ever since I was a youngster I had dreamed of owning a ranch. I liked every aspect of ranch work and fully sympathized with my son, Joe, who at one time had wanted to be a cowboy.

Eventually, a glimmer of this dream became a reality when Jeannette and I visited some friends in their small vacation home on a lake in the Deer Lake Estates development near Wimberley. We fell in love with the area and bought about nine lakeside acres on which we built a small house.

Our family spent many happy weekends there. The following year we heard that three hundred and fifty acres on the other side of the lake were being sold by the Deer Lake developers. The rolling hills were covered with groves of cedar, live oak, Spanish oak, wild cherry, and elm. It was a wilderness in which we could often spot deer bounding through the trees—and catch the flash of wild turkeys.

Looking at it from a vantage point one day, I found myself lost in its beauty. Jeannette squeezed my arm.

"You like it, don't you?"

"Yes, how about you?"

"I think we could be very happy here."

We bought the land in 1950, and later build a large rock barn and a comfortable ranch house on top of a hill with a swimming pool in the front yard. We found it a wonderful

place in which to relax and eventually added more outbuild-
ings including some stables. All three of our children became
good riders, and when Joanie was in her early teens she began
riding gaited horses and won several honors in horse shows.

We named our place the Circle J, signifying the Jaworski
family circle. This circle widened as our children went on to
college and brought their friends home with them. The ranch
rang with fun-filled activities: galloping horses, swimmers
splashing in the pool, and gustatory exclamations at the bar-
becue pit. It probably became one of the most active play-
grounds in Texas.

Even so, the ranch was a weekend place, and when we
moved to a larger house in the city I wanted it to be as close to
the office as practical. We found one in an area of Houston that
was only a fifteen-minute drive from downtown. The two-
story red brick colonial with three bedrooms had a small
garden in which Jeannette took great delight growing azaleas
and camellias.

Back in downtown Houston I was becoming more and more
involved in community activities. In 1949 I had been elected
president of the Houston Bar Association, and a year later
became president of the Texas Civil Judicial Council, which
among other things advises the governor, legislature, and
courts on matters regarding the improvement of the administration of justice.

If my self-esteem was elevated by these honors, I was
brought back to reality in June, 1950.

It all started when the president of the Houston School
Board decided—without my approval—to submit my name as
a nominee for a vacancy on the board.

I had not sought a place on the school board, since I knew
that some board members and I held varying views. I had
often spoken out on behalf of the underdog, and had made my
opinions known on everything from fair employment to race
relations.

In short, some people considered me a liberal. Actually I
had only sided with so-called "liberals" when I thought they

were right. I had seen enough of extremism in Nazi Germany to convince me that one should be moderate in forming one's views.

I told the president that my appointment by the board might seem to indicate that I would automatically support the policies and practices now being advocated by certain board members, with which I did not agree. If appointed, I told him, I would continue to speak out for what I believed to be right.

Even so, the school board president placed my name in nomination, Friday, June 2. It was a day I'll never forget.

The Friday evening Houston *Chronicle* carried the news in a front-page headline: TWO TAKE SCHOOL BOARD WALK-OUT. The headline even overshadowed the news about a plot to kill General MacArthur. Another headline read: TWO MEMBERS STORM OUT AFTER JAWORSKI IS URGED FOR VACANCY.

"Two members of the board," the news story reported, "red-faced and angry, stalked out of a school board meeting today when the board president recommended a candidate for a board vacancy in open session.

"The two board members jumped to their feet and headed for the door seconds after attorney Leon Jaworski was nominated."

The walkout started a debacle that raged in subsequent board meetings for weeks—with all of it headlined in the Houston newspapers and carried on television and in radio announcements.

I didn't even enjoy walking down the street anymore, though many well-meaning friends assured me they felt some school board members were behaving stupidly.

The controversy reached a peak on June 13 when banner headlines in the Houston *Post* screamed: CITY SCHOOL BOARD REJECTS JAWORSKI. Even though I had specifically requested that my name not be considered, they had gone ahead and voted on me anyway. My appointment was turned down by a four-to-two vote. A reason given for rejection was that one of my law firm's partners served on the bank that the schools used for deposits and loans. However, the same school board member making this charge later recommended a vice-president of this bank to fill the vacancy.

In any event I wished that I had never heard of the school board. My ego had been crushed and I prayed for understanding and the strength to forget it.

Not long after this I became even more active in civic and professional activities in which I felt I could better serve my community. Later, I was elected chairman of the local Red Cross chapter and then president of the downtown Rotary Club, the largest club of its kind in the world. I got so busy I forgot the school board debacle.

In 1954 Oma died. She had not been well and Hannibal had taken her to the hospital in Waco. Late one night we got the telephone call; she had died of a stroke.

I was heartbroken over the loss of this shy, gentle woman who had truly been a mother to us all when we desperately needed one. At the graveside in the little cemetery in Geronimo I thanked God for allowing her and my father to meet.

I looked at the little church across the way and thought how much this country chapel had come to mean to me. In memory I could again see my father earnestly preaching from the pulpit, and Hannibal furiously pumping the organ pedals as the congregation sang.

Now there were four dear ones—mama, Joe, papa, and Oma—who were buried in the graveyard across the road. In the next years I found myself returning to Geronimo to visit the cemetery and the little church, sometimes with Jeannette, sometimes alone. Often I would enter the sanctuary to meditate about the past and present. As I sat there—sometimes during a weekday when I was the only one in the pews—I would think of the message of Burris A. Jenkins: "With all its faults, I love the church because it is the chief dwelling place on earth of my Master and my Saviour."

It is not only nostalgia that brought me back nor the debt that I felt I owed this little church. Someone once said that if you really want to sort out your life, you should return to your roots. Mine were here in this little country church.

I know now, as Alexis de Tocqueville had realized after his visit to our land in its early days, that America's greatness lies in such churches.

In 1831 the French government sent de Tocqueville to examine our prisons and penitentiaries. But he became intrigued by our system of government and its institutions and therefore devoted considerable time to analyzing life in America.

On his return de Tocqueville wrote his classic, *Democracy in America,* which scholars feel is probably the greatest book on any national policy and culture.

In it he said:

I sought for the greatness and genius of America in her commodious harbors and her ample rivers, and it was not there . . . .

I sought for the greatness and genius of America in her democratic congress and her matchless constitution, and it was not there.

Not until I went into the churches of America and heard her pulpits flame with righteousness did I understand the secret of her genius and power.

America is great because America is good, and if America ever ceases to be good, America will cease to be great.

De Tocqueville did not attribute America's greatness to the power vested in the executive branch, or to the power lodged in the legislature, or to the authority and jurisdiction of the judiciary. Not even, to our "matchless constitution." He regarded these as what they are—the processes and means whereby good government can be achieved. But these processes are all administered by human beings and are subject to human error and frailty. He looked beyond the visible structure of government and went deeper to observe the foundation on which the edifice was built.

In America he saw a foundation of morality, which led her to greatness. In light of this unmistakable truth he admonished the then generation of Americans as well as generations to come: "If America ever ceases to be good, America will cease to be great."

The guardian of such goodness is the church. Our pulpits must flame with righteousness in order for this morality to exist. Unfortunately, today, some of them fall short because the pastors feel inhibited. It seems to be much the same kind of timidity that turned to cowardice in Nazi Germany and led the ministers to stifle their devotion to truth, except for a few who spoke for God.

But even in our country today it is difficult to solely blame pastors for this. In my father's day, ministers could lower the boom on their congregations and people accepted their remonstrances without retaliation. Many may have stamped home from church grumbling to themselves, but eventually they often took to heart what was preached.

But today's pastor, in too many cases, has to be very careful of what he says from the pulpit. Unfortunately, there always seem to be certain strong financial pillars of the congregation who indicate their displeasure if they disagree with the minister's preaching. They find ways of intimating that the preacher is "meddling," instead of preaching, even though they are usually the ones who most need the message. Too often these people succeed in muffling vital truths that should be heard.

When public issues are discussed from the pulpit, especially at election time, reactionaries often charge that this violates the doctrine of separation of church and state. They misunderstand the doctrine. One of the aims of our constitution was to preserve freedom of religion. Our Supreme Court zealously guards this provision, and any attempt to legislate a burden on the free exercise of religious beliefs—or antireligious beliefs, or on no beliefs—would be stricken down.

The constitutional guarantee of these rights does not impinge on the minister's prerogative to preach on political issues. In fact, the Constitution's protection of freedom of speech gives him that right.

Critics of the church's freedom to participate in political discussions point to the tax exemptions it enjoys. But these are granted by the taxing authorities and the government can take these exemptions away at any time it chooses.

Of course, I feel a minister should not devote pulpit time to discussing pure politics. But if conditions in the community exist that are contrary to the teachings of Jesus Christ, it is his duty to relate them to God's Word. Unfortunately, all too often he is unable to buck the tide of adverse sentiments in his congregation. He faces failure if he takes too strong a stand—the dismal prospect of moving his family elsewhere and all the other problems that go along with "losing a church." I believe the sin of inhibiting the pastor from full and free discussion of subjects that affect the spiritual life of the community is tantamount to suppressing the Word of God.

There is hardly a one of us, I feel, who does not squirm in his pew at one time or another when we hear God's Word. But if the time ever comes when a pastor can no longer factually discuss mankind's sins without hindrance, worshiping in church will have lost its purpose.

There was no danger of this happening at First Presbyterian Church in Houston. Dr. Charles King had a way of pointing out truths that made many of us uneasy.

One day he came to my office to point out a truth that made me squirm in a most uncomfortable way.

12
Condemned to Death

It was a beautiful May afternoon in 1958 when I became involved in a most unusual criminal case that I shall remember for the rest of my life.

I was just returning to my office from lunch when my secretary flagged me down. "Dr. King called," she said. "He wants to come over as soon as posible, says it's extremely urgent."

"Tell him to come ahead," I answered.

Sitting at my desk I wondered what my pastor was so concerned about. It wasn't like him to get overly excited. Dr. Charles L. King was my close friend and I always looked forward to seeing him. A tall, dynamic man and a great, forceful speaker, he always wore a black felt hat that had become something of a trademark.

Within thirty minutes Dr. King was in my office. "Leon, a real tragedy has happened," he said, tossing his black hat on a table and dropping his lanky frame in a chair. "A man not responsible for his actions has been convicted of murder and sentenced to death!"

I had never seen my friend so concerned. Still puzzled at what he wanted, I urged him to continue.

"The man is Ron Cooper*, the brother of a good friend of mine who's a great servant of the Lord and one of the most dedicated Presbyterian ministers in the state," he said, wiping his brow. His eyes behind thick-lensed glasses showed pain as he continued. "This tragedy has broken his brother's heart and crushed everyone in the family. Leon, imagine your own brother going to the electric chair when he doesn't even realize what he's done!"

I nodded sympathetically, still wondering what my friend wanted.

Dr. King took a breath and continued. "Just this morning the Court of Criminal Appeals of Texas affirmed the death sentence. I have conferred with other lawyers, and they suggested that we seek your assistance."

I leaned forward, my elbows on the desk, wondering what I could do that had not already been done.

"I'm sorry to put it so bluntly, Leon, but his family doesn't have the funds to employ you. As your pastor I have come to ask your help." He sat back, his eyes questioning me.

What he had just told me sounded like a hopeless case. I took off my glasses and cleaned them with a handkerchief. "Is he represented by counsel?"

"Yes, he has a lawyer, a good one, and I'm here with his counselor's knowledge and consent."

"Can you tell me anything more about the case?"

Dr. King leaned forward in his chair. "Well, I don't know all the details, but this man's wife had died and—why I don't know—he beat his elderly mother-in-law to death with a vase. He was arrested the same day and made a written statement confessing the killing. Feeling against him ran high in the

*The actual name has been changed.

132

community, and they tried him as soon as possible—fourteen days later."

"Didn't his lawyer try for a continuance?"

"Yes, but it was overruled. The poor man's only defense was insanity. However, a state psychiatrist who examined him found him sane. The tragedy is that Ron Cooper was discharged from the army because of mental trouble, but they couldn't locate his discharge records in time for the trial."

My friend stared at the floor. "So his insanity defense couldn't be developed, and the poor, demented man was sentenced to death. Now the Court of Criminal Appeals has affirmed it." He settled back in his chair, shaking his head.

This was one time I wished my friend had stuck to ecclesiastical matters. "But I just don't see how I can be of any help," I began. "In the first place I'm not practicing criminal law now. But more importantly, the Court of Criminal Appeals is the court of last resort in Texas, and it has affirmed the conviction and sentence."

I looked at him levelly. "The court seldom changes its decision, Dr. King. You're asking me to shut the gate after the horses are out." I leaned back in my chair and sighed. "On top of it all, I'm extremely busy now. I just don't see how I can take on something that would require me to drop almost everything else and prepare a motion for rehearing in a matter with which I'm totally unfamiliar."

My pastor stared at me for a moment. He slowly rose from his chair, picked up his black hat, and walked to the door. As he opened it he turned, and said, "Well, Leon, it is between you and the Lord."

Time stood still for a moment. The responsibility was awesome.

"Wait a minute, Dr. King," I found myself blurting, "let me think it over."

He hesitated at the door.

"Who has the record of the proceedings?" I asked lamely.

"It's with his lawyer."

"Can I see it as soon as possible?"

"Tomorrow," he said and slipped out the door.

For some time after Dr. King left I sat there pondering the situation. My views on capital punishment had changed since I was an impatient young lawyer just starting out in Waco. At the time I had thought that without exception the death penalty was barbaric. Once, in court, I had concealed a stiletto in my coat pocket. Walking over to the jury box I said, "If you're going to send this man to the electric chair, you might as well step right over to him and stab him now."

Whipping out the stiletto, I tried to hand it to one of the jurors who almost fainted.

Even now, many years after the Ron Cooper case, I'm still not so sure about it. I remember how I had tried to find something in the Bible that was explicit about the death penalty. Yet even though many people who advocate the death sentence have cited excerpts from the Old Testament favoring it, authoritative religious leaders are not in accord with this. And in the New Testament, Christ did not treat the subject definitively as far as I can see.

But after looking over statistics and studying states with and without the penalty in recent years, I have finally come to believe that the death sentence serves as a deterrent to some crimes. There is currently a growing number of cases where a robber or rapist murders his victim in cold blood to avoid identification, or even for the sheer perverse delight of killing.

An average of one violent personal crime is committed every thirty seconds in the United States and one property crime every three seconds, according to the FBI Uniform Crime Report, published in 1978. Such violence is beginning to have its effect.

Fear of crime has changed the life-styles of the majority of people throughout the country, a recent survey reported.* Six out of ten people say they dress plainly to avoid being noticed

*The Figgie Report on Fear of Crime, conducted by Research and Forecasts, Inc., 1980.

by criminals. Four in ten Americans are highly fearful they will become victims of violent crimes such as murder, rape, robbery, or assault, and feel unsafe in their homes, neighborhoods, workplaces, or shopping centers. Two in three Americans favor the death penalty for convicted murderers.

I think of the highway patrolmen in my state who have politely approached drivers stopped for a traffic violation only to be met by a blazing gun. In the ten years between 1969 and 1978, 1,123 law officers were slain in our nation by criminals; in some instances the murderer had stood over the prostrate body and emptied his gun into vital parts.

In such cases and in others equally as abominable I favor the death penalty if the jury deems it appropriate. I feel that it would act as a deterrent to those who may be tempted to commit these crimes.

But I have always felt gravely concerned about the possibility of the penalty taking the life of an innocent individual. It should be approved only where ample evidence is unmistakably clear and convincing.

To me, this was clearly the case with Ron Cooper, a man who was not rational, who should not be held responsible for what he did. For if there is any possibility that the condemned man is of unsound mind, then the death sentence is wrong. This is the law of our land.

Yet, back in that spring of 1958, as I pondered the case before me, I did not see how the death penalty could possibly be changed. The highest court in our state had affirmed the sentence, and at that time the United States Supreme Court was not open to appeals of this kind.

As I sat there turning a pencil over and over in my hand, a small voice seemed to speak within me. *The Most High Counselor can do it. And he can be reached through prayer.*

The next morning the trial transcript arrived, and I asked my secretary to hold all calls. I read and reread it, including the opinion of the appellate court. When I stopped to rest my eyes, I kept hearing the words of my pastor: "Well, Leon, it is between you and the Lord."

After I had finished studying the transcript, it still seemed hopeless. But folding my hands on it, I asked the Lord for guidance, strength, and the wisdom to do right. *Father, I prayed, grant me the courage to do what needs to be done. Keep me steadfast, firm in purpose, resolute in faith.*

And then I went to work.

After sifting the evidence for several hours, I called the attorney who had been handling the appeal. An experienced criminal lawyer, he expressed hope that I would enter the case.

"I look forward to working with you," I replied, adding that I wanted to contact the other lawyers mentioned by Dr. King who were willing to sign my brief in support of a motion for rehearing.

With their approval, I contacted the presiding justice of the Court of Criminal Appeals in the state capitol in Austin asking permission for these lawyers to appear as "friends of the court." I also asked the court to allow us fifteen days to file a brief that would give our written argument.

Before giving an answer, the presiding judge would have to confer with the two other judges of the court. There would be a wait.

I headed for our ranch where I released the tension by cutting firewood. This was a hobby I had started after finding a number of dead trees on our land. It offered a twofold benefit: fuel for the fireplaces of my family and much-needed exercise for myself. On top of this I found it relaxing therapy after tension-filled days in trial court.

A few days later we received news that the request had been granted. Working as fast as possible to keep within the short time limit, we prepared a brief in support of our motion, pointing out that Ron Cooper's trial should have been delayed until the vital army records attesting to his mental aberration arrived. Our brief closed with the question: "Does not justice demand that the defendant be given a trial in which the facts pertinent to his mental condition are fully and fairly developed?"

Months went by as we waited.

Then came a set back. On November 5, 1958, the Court of Criminal Appeals denied our motion for a rehearing. However, the presiding judge dissented from the other two judges. He began his statement with the words: "After more careful study, I find that I cannot agree to the affirmation of this death-penalty conviction."

This gave us a slim hope—albeit one hanging by a thin thread. The dissenting opinion meant that the court would consider a second motion for a rehearing. I breathed a prayer of thanks for the condemned man's new lease on life and again obtained permission for the lawyers to appear *amici curiae* in support of the second motion for a rehearing.

This would be Ron Cooper's last chance.

We prepared and filed another brief and then waited. On March 25, 1959, almost a year after Dr. King had come to my office, our second motion was granted, and by a two-to-one decision the judgment of the Court of Criminal Appeals was reversed, paving the way for a new trial.

Then something happened that I believe could only be the result of the Holy Spirit at work. Both the state psychiatrist who had originally found the man sane and the district attorney who had called for the death sentence admitted their mistakes and concluded that a man not responsible for his actions had been tried for murder. Instead of another trial, a sanity hearing was held. The state psychiatrist reexamined the defendant and found him insane. As a resut, Ron Cooper was confined to a mental institution.

A day later a letter from his grateful brother came thanking me on behalf of the family: "May God richly bless you in your work and in his service." In the same mail was a letter from Dr. King. He wrote: "I firmly believe that in helping him, you have helped his Lord and your Lord."

As I look back on what I feel was a miracle, I believe that the prayers of Ron Cooper's family, his friends, Dr. King's, and my own were answered.

Something powerful happened that saved this man from an

unjust and ignominious death and spared his family heartbreaking agony. For there was no unusual persuasion on my part or that of anyone else associated with this appeal, and the legal issues remained the same from the onset.

I firmly believe it was a case, pure and simple, of the influence of God's Holy Spirit. By being obedient to him, my role was merely that of an instrument.

Thus in contrast to the vengeful atmosphere of the first trial, the authorities were impelled to be Christlike in justice, patience, and compassion. In the end they applied the judicial process of the United States Consitution as it was meant to operate.

I often think of Ron Cooper when controversy on the death penalty arises as it so often does these days. Almost six years after this case, President Lyndon Johnson established the Commission on Law Enforcement and Administration of Justice in response to an anxious nation's crime problem.

I served on this commission along with a large number of judges, lawyers, law enforcement officers, and civic leaders. In February of 1967 we released our general report, *The Challenge of Crime in Free Society*.

The Commission recommended:

> The question whether capital punishment is an appropriate sanction is a policy decision to be made by each state. Where it is retained, the types of offenses for which it is available should be strictly limited, and the law should be enforced in an evenhanded and nondiscriminatory manner, with procedures for review of death sentences that are fair and expeditious.

This recommendation underlined my own feelings. If it had been followed in Ron Cooper's case, he and his family would not have lived under such a terrible burden for many months.

It is tragic that in our society we seem to have a need for the death penalty in certain limited instances. My prayer is that we as a national family reach that stage of development where it can be abandoned completely.

When I think back over Ron Cooper's case, I have to admit that he would have gone to the electric chair if it hadn't been for one lone minister who made one of his congregation squirm. Thanks to Dr. Charles King I was again taught that "with God, all things are possible."

Some days after this case was settled, I headed out into the hills at the Circle J to be alone for a while. I had driven far into the back country with my jeep and chain saw to find some firewood. But the air was so crisp and the panorama of hills and woods so beautiful that I found myself sitting on a stump just enjoying my surroundings. A pungency of cedar filled the air and I felt a deep peace filling my heart.

As I think back to that moment, I am so grateful that God does not let us see into the future. For as I relaxed in his beautiful world, I had no idea that I would be facing probably one of the most turbulent times in our nation's history, when law and its proper order would be in deep crisis.

13
The Battle of Ole Miss

The screams of wounded men swelled with the roar of gunfire as government police fought back an enraged mob at the university. One man's head shot back, a rifle slug exploding his forehead. A news correspondent fell facedown in the grass, a bullet between his shoulder blades.

Standing in the light of overturned blazing autos, a glassy-eyed ex-army general harangued the rioters into greater fury. Meanwhile local government leaders trembled in the background.

An early "putsch" of the National Socialist party in Germany? A revolutionists' takeover in a South American country?

No, it was the campus of a major university in the United States on September 30, 1962.

As Jeannette and I sat in our Houston living room watching television, the newscaster said that this struggle had become the most serious confrontation between state and federal authority since the Civil War.

We glanced at each other, aghast at the scene that was being played out before our eyes. But we had no way of knowing that I would soon become personally involved in this bitter conflict, nor did we realize how much we would suffer from it until almost two months later.

My involvement began on a gray mid-November afternoon in 1962. I had just returned to my office from lunch when my secretary buzzed me on the intercom. "It's Mr. Katzenbach, deputy attorney general," she said.

Wondering what the Justice Department of the United States wanted of me I picked up the phone. Nick Katzenbach, whom I knew, came straight to the point.

Would I help prosecute Ross Barnett, the governor of Mississippi?

I was a bit stunned. Why did the Justice Department decide to call me?

The deputy attorney general went on to say that I had been recommended by prominent members of the American Bar Association. He added that I had also been approved by Elbert Tuttle, chief judge of the Fifth Circuit Court of Appeals, which had jurisdiction over the university.

"Would you come to Washington to discuss it further?" he asked.

I shrank from the idea; the situation was a hornet's nest. But I felt that I should at least discuss it with them. The following day I boarded a plane at the Houston airport.

As the jet airplane rose in the sky I settled back into my seat to think about the situation in which Nick Katzenbach wished me to become involved. It had all started almost two years ago when James Meredith, a quiet, twenty-nine-year-old black Mississippian with nine years' air force service, had decided to transfer from an all-Negro college to his state's university. But by class time in September of 1962, the University of Mississippi had made it quite clear that it was not about to be integrated.

In denying his admission, the local district judge had found "as a fact, that the university is not a racially segregated institution." He claimed that though segregation was the custom before the Supreme Court's 1954 landmark ruling against the practice, "there is no custom or policy now, nor was there any at the time of the plaintiff's applications, which excluded Negroes from entering the university."

I had raised my eyebrows at this claim, having been told that the only blacks on the Ole Miss campus were custodians and kitchen help.

Meredith's case was heard in the district court, the court of appeals, and then the United States Supreme Court. With all its legal remedies exhausted, the state of Mississippi was ordered by the Fifth Circuit Court to admit Meredith.

However, bitter-end segregationists vowed to resist. Striding to the fore as their champion was Mississippi Governor Ross Barnett.

In mid-September of 1962, he had sat in the Ole Miss auditorium as the slightly built Meredith stood before him seeking admission. Outside the ivy-covered building, grounds keepers had picked up charred remnants of three crosses burned some nights before.

"Your application has been refused," Barnett snapped, defying two United States government court orders.

He had invoked the old doctrine of "interposition," claiming that for order and safety he had to "interpose and invoke the police powers of the state."

However the United States Court of Appeals held this to be constitutionally groundless. The old states' rights doctrine that a federal law can be voided within its own borders had been struck down long ago, pragmatically by the Civil War and legally by U.S. Supreme Court decisions.

Governor Barnett was ordered to appear before the Court of Appeals in New Orleans to answer charges of civil contempt.

He stayed in Mississippi.

As I followed his defiance, I could not help but compare him to General Andrew Jackson, another southerner. After his great victory over the British at the Battle of New Orleans in the War of 1812, Old Hickory somewhat high-handedly kept the militia under arms and New Orleans under martial law when public officials no longer thought it necessary.

The governor and the legislature greatly resented his stubborn ways. A series of unpleasant incidents resulted in a $1,000 fine imposed on Jackson by a federal judge for contempt of court.

Instead of ducking it, Andrew Jackson, crusty as he was, entered the courtroom with dignity and paid the fine. Moreover, when overeager supporters launched a demonstration in his favor, he quickly quelled it, advising his friends to recognize the supremacy of the law.

In Governor Barnett's case, the court tried him in absentia, found him guilty, and gave him four days to "purge himself" by simply doing as he had been ordered. It set a fine of $10,000 a day and confinement in the custody of the U.S. attorney general if he did not comply.

Despite this Barnett and his lieutenant governor, Paul Johnson, Jr., turned James Meredith away from the Ole Miss campus two more times.

With each rejection more of the citizenry deluded themselves into thinking that their defiance would be a turning point in the battle for states' rights against the "unchecked might of central government." Extremists began taking advantage of their hour, setting the stage for open rebellion. In many a white Mississippian's heart the historic cry for near-secession undoubtedly struck a responsive chord.

But Barnett's new popularity had perched him on the horns of a dilemma. His office had become a pawn in an explosive situation fast running out of control.

As my plane droned on toward Washington I didn't realize that behind the scenes Barnett had resigned himself to the inevitability of Meredith's admission. Later that morning when I finally reached Washington, Robert Kennedy would reveal to me the private conversations he and President John F. Kennedy had had with Ross Barnett.

For during the last days of September, 1962, the telephone wires between Barnett and the Kennedys had grown hot. By Saturday, September 29, Barnett had seemed to be looking for a face-saving way out.

"I've got to have a show of force," he said. " . . . If I were overwhelmed . . ."

The next day President Kennedy signed papers federalizing the Mississippi National Guard and moving regular army troops to Memphis on standby.

In a phone conversation with Barnett that morning, Robert Kennedy believed the governor hinted that it might be best to bring Meredith to the gates of Ole Miss that day.

"Then they (the Federal marshals) should point their guns at us, and then we could step aside," Barnett suggested. Soon U.S. marshals in company with Deputy Attorney General Nicholas Katzenbach escorted Meredith to the college.

As the 320 marshals took up posts around the campus, a state police officer insisted, "The people around here are deeply religious, and nothing will make them madder than registering Meredith on a Sunday."

Already a small crowd of students had gathered to jeer the federal marshals as they ushered the would-be student to a dormitory where he would spend the longest night of his life.

The crowd swelled and by seven o'clock in the evening students and joiners-in fired their first barrage of the battle of Ole Miss—first spitting, then throwing pebbles, and finally hurling rocks. Someone set a U.S. Army truck on fire.

The wavering Governor Barnett pled for Mississippians to keep the peace. "My heart still says 'never,' " he said, "but my calm judgment abhors the bloodshed that would follow."

President Kennedy, on nationwide tv and radio, bent over backwards in praising Mississippi and its role in U.S. history. He did not raise a moral argument for integration but rested his case on respect for the law.

"Americans are free to disagree with the law, but not to disobey it," he said. "For in a government of laws, and not of men, no man, however prominent or powerful, and no mob, however unruly or boisterous, is entitled to defy a court of law.

"If this country should ever reach the point where any man or group of men by force or threat of force," he continued, "could long deny the commands of our court and our Constitution, then no law would stand free from doubt, no judge would be sure of his writ, and no citizen would be safe from his neighbors."

However, those in the mushrooming mob on the Ole Miss campus decided to follow their own law.

More joined them as outsiders began streaming into the university town of Oxford. A "preacher" drove up from Florida with four revolvers and four high-powered rifles. A grizzled Alabamian led thirty men in six sedans from Mobile to "fight for our Constitution." On reaching Oxford, he asked, "Where is that there school?"

As the campus darkened into night and the hate flamed higher, the now two thousand rioters spilled out of control. The confrontation that I watched on tv became history. Rocks and metal bars were hurled at the marshals who began falling back, some stunned and wounded. Finally the order was given for tear gas. As eye-stinging clouds billowed into the night, the crowd scattered screaming, "You --- ------ communists!" "You nigger-lovers go to ----!"

Re-forming, the mob like some enraged animal now roared back at the marshals who crouched behind cars as flaming bottles of gasoline burst into lakes of fire around them. The Ole Miss campus had become a battleground.

Above the angry howls of the mob and the popping of tear-gas canisters could be heard the hoarse voice of an ex-major general of the United States Army, Edwin A. Walker, who had rushed to the fray from his home in Texas.

Standing at the foot of the Confederate soldier statue, he spurred the young students on, shouting, "Don't let up now!" His eyes staring wildly, he screamed, "You may lose this battle but you will have to be heard. . . . You must be prepared for possible death."

Five years earlier this same army officer had led troops sent by President Eisenhower into Little Rock, Arkansas, to control the school integration crisis there. He had since resigned his commission after being admonished for extreme right-wing talk. He had come to Jackson crying for Americans "from every state" to march to Barnett's aid, proclaiming that the court orders were part of "the conspiracy of the crucifixion by anti-Christ conspirators of the Supreme Court."

Now students rushed up to him for battle strategy advice.

In the meantime more outsiders streamed onto the campus, toughs from surrounding states carrying rifles, shotguns, and knives. The madness flamed through the mob. A stolen bulldozer was sent rumbling toward the marshals but it crashed into a tree.

"We need a machine gun!" came a hysterical cry. Someone commandeered an old fire engine and, with rioters running behind it, charged the marshals.

Tear gas blunted the attack.

A shotgun roared, sending a slug through a marshal's neck. He was saved from bleeding to death by a local Oxford doctor.

The crack of snipers' rifles was accented by the whine of bullets ricocheting off ivy-covered walls. An onlooker standing at a campus gate fell dead with a bullet in his forehead.

Inside the Lyceum, the venerable administration building of the 114-year-old university, the government had set up its command post. One hundred years ago its floor had been bloodied by the wounded of both Confederate and Union troops. Now it was stained red again by marshals staggering in for first aid.

Crouched at one of the desks, phone in hand, an anxious Nick Katzenbach asked Washington for troops. Outside Mississippians were fighting Mississippians as troops from the state's National Guard arrived on the scene.

Thousands of flaming gasoline-filled bottles arced through the campus trees setting more cars and shrubbery ablaze.

Shortly before midnight Barnett spoke on the radio. "I call

on all Mississippians to keep the faith and courage. We will never surrender."

The battle raged through the night. Again and again the supply of tear gas, the only defense used by federal marshals against the mob, would fall dangerously low. And again and again army trucks roared in with more.

Finally army trucks and jeeps filled with hundreds of troops rumbled toward the "front" from Memphis. Near Oxford a convoy was stoned by a mob lining the highway. Most of the men were struck by rocks and other hard objects and 128 windshields were smashed. But the convoy got through, and by 4:45 A.M. troops had set up positions in front of the Lyceum, M-14 rifles with bayonets at the ready.

Monday's sun rose to shine on a campus that looked like a World War II battleground littered with smoking wrecks of autos, thousands of broken bottles, and tattered sign cards emblazoned: "Ross Is Right."

One newscaster spoke of the campus glistening in the morning sun from myriads of glass fragments. I couldn't help but think of the *"Kristallnacht"* (Crystal Night) in early Nazi Germany when hoodlums supported by local authorities smashed windows of Jewish homes, shops, and synagogues, and the streets "gleamed like crystal" the next dawn.

Soon after sunup, Monday, Oxford was in a state of military rule, with troops patrolling the street and manning roadblocks. Along with captured rioters brought in for questioning was the ex-general Edwin Walker. Charged with insurrection, he was later flown to a medical center for psychiatric examination.

At 7:30 A.M. James H. Meredith was escorted into the Lyceum where he registered as a student at the University of Mississippi. A quiet settled on the campus and he began attending classes that week.

While the litter of rocks, bottles, rifle shells, and tear-gas canisters were being cleaned up, the U.S. attorney general had no recourse but to prosecute Governor Ross Barnett for criminal contempt.

On November 15, 1962, the United States Court of Appeals for the Fifth Circuit ordered that the attorney general of the United States, and attorneys he designated, prosecute criminal contempt proceedings against the governor and his lieutenant governor "to determine whether they are, or either of them is, guilty of criminal contempt of the orders of this court."

And this was why Nick Katzenbach had called me: to prosecute a governor who had openly defied the law of our land. But as my plane landed at Dulles Airport I was still unsure if I wanted to enter such an explosive situation.

A government car took me to the Justice Department building, where I was ushered into the office of Nick Katzenbach. After a brief visit, Nick introduced me to Burke Marshall, chief of the department's Civil Rights Division, and his eventual successor, John Doar.

Then we went to Robert Kennedy's office where Nick left the attorney general and me alone. There was an air of tension in the room, which was quickly offset when the lean wiry Kennedy flashed his brilliant smile and shook my hand.

"So glad to have you with us, counselor," he said in his broad Boston accent as he offered me a chair. After he outlined the situation I could see why his department had to bring in outside counsel. Robert Kennedy, himself, might have to testify to the telephone conversations he had had with Ross Barnett. He and the men directly under him could hardly prosecute a case in which they might be witnesses. As he spoke he paced the office, occasionally running a hand through his thick brown hair when he emphasized the seriousness of the situation. "The president and I have talked this over, and we both have decided that you are the appropriate one to act as prosecutor.

"We know it's a difficult and thankless task we're asking of you," he said. Then he stared at me intently. "Will you take the case?"

It was deadly quiet in the room; I could sense my heart beating rapidly. My mind raced. There were so many complexities in this case: it was more than a legal argument; it was a battle of cultures, of philosophies.

"Please let me think it over," I asked. "I need a little time, but I'll let you know as soon as possible."

"Would you like to see the president and talk with him?"

"No, I don't think it is necessary," I replied. "I know he's very busy, and you've given me all the information I need to make a decision."

Robert Kennedy nodded, we shook hands, and I went back to Burke Marshall's office where he and John Doar gave me a detailed briefing on the facts of the case.

After learning what I needed to know about the criminal contempt proceeding, I was on my way back to the airport.

My homeward-bound plane flew high above the clouds. As I gazed through the port down to their cottony expanse, I felt removed from the earth. To me it was symbolic. As a lawyer I could view the Mississippi situation dispassionately. A court order had been defied flagrantly, and without the upholding of court orders, our laws could not be enforced.

Yet, as my plane roared on to Houston, I knew that underneath the clouds was the earth. And within a couple of hours I would be walking on it. I would have to live in reality. I would have to face the fact that my roots were in Texas, a state very much a part of the South.

Yet I knew that Southern tradition must have no part in my decision. Mine had to be based on the law of our country. Moreover if court decrees are to be flouted, there soon would be no law—in the South or elsewhere.

As the jet engines roared on toward the setting sun I found myself going back to the origins of the law of our land. I went back even further, to the basics, that all real laws emanate from God. We know that God set up the laws of matter and motion, the cause of order in the universe.

The venerated eighteenth-century sage of English law, Blackstone, said in his *Commentaries*. "Man . . . must necessarily be subject to the laws of his Creator. . . . This will of his Maker is called the law of nature."

Yet, I knew that men, granted free will by the Creator, disobeyed the laws of nature and of God. So society must necessarily have rules. The first laws were given by God himself: the Ten Commandments, which had established principles of just and moral behavior throughout history.

I leaned my head back on my seat and thought how God had shaped the spirit of America, and how he had so often been invoked in the crucial development of our country's political society. From the time the Pilgrims first knelt on American soil to thank God for his guidance and ask his blessings on their adventure, I deeply believe that faith in him has played an integral part in directing our nation's destiny. Our trust in God has been both our spiritual sustenance and guidance and, in our darkest hours, he has been our beacon of hope.

I thought back to when I had stood in Philadelphia's Independence Hall where our Constitution was drafted, the very document that was now under attack in Mississippi.

I remembered having visualized in my mind's eye that room in 1787 where four months of intense debate, deliberation, and study had gone into an attempt to forge a system of government that would meet the varying needs of all parts of America.

Even then there was great dissension—shouting, arguing men with vast differences of opinions that represented an already complex country. A number of different plans for the Constitution had been submitted, but the Convention came very close to breaking down over an argument between the large states and the small states, whose representatives worried about unfair representation.

"The greatest difficulty lies in the affair of representation," wrote James Madison, "and if this could be adjusted, all others would be surmountable."

As the tension mounted and as hot and angry words flew back and forth it looked as if the entire convention would break up.

Finally on a hot day late in June when the controversy flamed highest, Benjamin Franklin, then eighty-one, a wise patriarch who had said little during the convention, lifted his aged body from his chair, took off his spectacles, and addressed the assemblage with these words:

In this situation of this Assembly, groping as it were in the dark to find political truth, and scarcely able to distinguish it when presented to us, how has it happened, Sir, that we have not hitherto once thought of humbly applying to the Father of lights, to illuminate our understanding?

In the beginning of the contest with Great Britain, when we were sensible of danger, we had daily prayer in this room for the Divine protection. Our prayers, Sir, were heard, and they were graciously answered.

All of us who are engaged in the struggle must have observed frequent instances of a superintending Providence in our favor. To that kind Providence we owe this happy opportunity of consulting in peace on the means of establishing our future national felicity. And have we now forgotten that powerful friend?

Do we imagine that we no longer need his assistance?

I have lived, Sir, a long time, and the longer I live, the more convincing proofs I see of this truth—that God governs in the affairs of men. And if a sparrow cannot fall to the ground without his notice, is it probable that an empire can rise without his aid? We have been assured, Sir, in the sacred writings, that "except the Lord build the house they labor in vain that build it."

Although Franklin's motion was not adopted, for fear that if failures did occur, the public would become even more alarmed, historians record that not only Franklin but others who heard his appeal spent time in individual prayer.

Not long after Franklin's impassioned plea, Roger Sherman proposed his "Connecticut Compromise," calling for a congress of two houses—one where each state had equal representation and another where representation was based on population.

As our airliner banked for its approach to the Houston airport, I thought about the problem now menacing the basis

CROSSROADS

of our Constitution. I was even more convinced that if a United States citizen was allowed to choose which laws or court orders to obey and which to defy, it could erode our system of government.

To say that one is justified in ignoring the law if his conscience speaks to the contrary is the same as saying that the rule of law is not to be the yardstick of our society's conduct. If a segregationist disobeys a law because it offends his moral belief of what is right, then will a civil rights leader not feel free to do the same?

And if an exception is tolerated, where is the line drawn? A conscientious objector to the income tax, for example, might find such a philosophy quite appealing. The inevitable result would be to weaken the foundation on which our system of law and order rests.

The very court whose order Governor Barnett flouted opens every session as does every other United States trial and appellate court with the prayer, "God save the United States and this honorable court."

Surely God wants this court saved, I thought. Yet, how can this and our other courts be saved in the face of such defiances? The answer was clear: If we do nothing about such defiances, they will certainly escalate and soon the rule of law will have lost its force and the rights and liberties of all of us will be imperiled.

By the time our plane had touched down in Houston I had made up my mind. I would accept the task that had been urged upon me.

My decision raised another question in my mind. At the time I was serving as president of the State Bar of Texas. I felt sure that some members would not approve of my acting as a prosecutor of Governor Barnett in this decisive racial confrontation.

Should I resign my office? I wondered.

After carefully thinking it over, I decided not to resign. If I did, it might be interpreted as a tacit admission on my part that the prosecution of Ross Barnett was not consistent with the views of the Texas bar. Also, I feared that many outsiders would conclude that I had been pressured to resign.

However, it was not the Texas bar that I should have been concerned about. It was the reaction of friends, acquaintances, and other members of the community who would soon descend upon me in full fury.

14
A Lonely Walk

Saturday, December 22, 1962, turned out to be one of the most hectic and grievous days of my life.

Because rumors about my appointment as prosecutor on the Governor Barnett case began to leak out, Attorney General Robert Kennedy announced my appointment much sooner than he had intended.

I had been at my office briefly that Saturday morning, but went home at noon because I had tickets for the Bluebonnet Bowl football game in the afternoon. On my way home both of Houston's afternoon papers were headlining the appointment, and the television and radio stations were buzzing with the news.

At home Jeannette said our phone had been ringing constantly. Worse, I could not believe the calls. Some friends wailed in anguish over my "betrayal" of the South, strangers bitterly denounced me, and cranks threatened my life.

"No matter what you do," I said to Jeannette, "you're bound to hear from the extremists and the misguided."

Finally we took the phone off the hook.

But our plans for the day and the evening would proceed as scheduled, we concluded. However, at the football game, we began to find out how widespread the emotional reaction had become. There were icy stares from people sitting around us, and some friends simply turned their heads away.

"I can't believe it," I muttered to Jeannette as we drove home. "They're all reasonable people. They should be able to understand what's really at stake there in Mississippi."

That evening we went to a party to which we had been invited some time ago by one of Houston's prominent citizens. Our hosts were friendly, but Jeannette and I often found ourselves standing alone. Other guests became very busy talking with each other when we happened by. We left earlier than usual, and as we waited for an attendant to bring our car, an oilman walked over to me and said quietly: "Leon, I have known you for over twenty-five years. Tonight is the first criticism I have heard of you, and it was sharp."

On our way home I mused to Jeannette: "It's just an initial reaction, honey. Perhaps after a few days everyone will get over it."

Then Jeannette caught her breath as we turned into our street. A police car was parked in front of the house.

"Sir," said an officer, "we have orders to guard your house for your protection."

In days following there were many bitter and angry letters in our mail. I threw all the anonymous mail into the wastebasket but answered those from friends who seemed genuinely disturbed.

A society matron and patron of the arts wrote that she was "distressed" to learn that I would prosecute Barnett. She said, "I cannot bear to see one of whom I am so fond fall in my estimation." Then she exhorted me "not to be a cat's paw to try to silence the eloquent voice of the fine old South." The final thrust on her perfumed stationery read: "Many of your friends and admirers are heart and soul for Barnett and believe what he is standing for far transcends any law of any court."

What really bothered me, however, was the attitude of many lawyers who blandly asserted that a Southerner who took part in the contempt proceedings was not only committing treason against the traditions of the South, but was wronging a "noble" governor.

The question of a payoff loomed in some minds. One judge, a friend, took me aside at a Bar Association meeting and asked pointedly, "What is it, Leon, the Supreme Court?"

I stared at him aghast. "I'm surprised and disappointed that you should even ask such a question!"

"Well," he said, glancing about guiltily, "you've been hurt, Leon, badly hurt by accepting, and . . ."

Probably the worst harassment was inflicted by the anonymous telephone callers, who spewed out hateful words the minute we answered the phone. I thought of another time when I was involved in an unpopular case, defending Jordan Scott in Waco, and we had the same type of calls.

These were sick people, I told Jeannette, and we should just forget them. But I wondered just how far such sickness extended when I got the following letter from the president of a mortgage and trust company in a nearby city: "Every mentally mature person knows that you are participating in the Mississippi affair to curry favor with the Administration and, probably, at the instructions of your bishop. I hope your daughter has a nigger baby."

I began to understand why many of the "good people" in Nazi Germany had succumbed to the power of peer pressure in those dark years. The thought kept recurring to me: Would I have stood up under the threats of death and torture that existed there?

It was times like these that I was especially grateful for the opportunity to retreat to our ranch. Little Mike, our daughter Joanie's son, joyfully went along with us. He was the first of our five grandsons; Claire had three boys and Joe had one. Now, due to strained circumstances in Joanie's life, Jeannette and I helped her take care of him.

I loved having a little boy again to bring to the playground in Houston where he'd laugh with glee as I pushed him on the swings, to take to the zoo where he'd beg for more peanuts to feed the monkeys, to hear his prayers at bedtime, and read to him as he fell asleep.

But most of all Mike loved our ranch. Joe, our son, had gone through law school, served in the army, and begun his own career. Now the joys that he and I had shared at the ranch belonged to Mike and me.

But all too soon, it seemed, I would have to be back in Houston where the controversy about my appointment continued to boil.

The state legislature was to convene within a few weeks, and I learned that a certain state senator planned to offer a resolution censuring me for serving as government counsel. He boasted that it would be the first resolution dropped into the hopper for 1963. Others who were more rational persuaded the senator not to present his resolution. Still the criticism continued.

Letters continued to flood our mailbox; many were from lawyers who were calling on me to resign as president of the Texas Bar Association. The chairman of the association's board was moved to poll the directors, and by a majority vote it was decided that no statements should be offered; they felt the matter should be regarded as personal.

Not all of the letters were negative. Many people commended me. But I was anguished to find that so many attorneys and sophisticated citizens failed to understand that Governor Barnett's act had struck directly at the supremacy of the law. Whether he was guilty of criminal contempt was not the issue of the moment. That would be determined later. The issue was the direction by a high court, the second highest in the land, that Barnett be charged and tried.

Despite assurances of support from those I deeply respected, in particular the senior partner of our law firm, John H. Crooker, Sr., I was still hurt by the messages of hate from individuals I had known well for years.

Hodding Carter, the Pulitzer Prize-winning author, once wrote, "Of course, no one enjoys—or should enjoy—unpopularity as such. But neither should we be afraid of making enemies." He cited an old Chinese proverb: "Just as tall trees are known by their shadows, so are good men known by their enemies."

But philosophical words were not enough for me. And again, when I found myself in troubled waters, I turned to my one real source of comfort and hope, the Bible.

I found myself rereading the Sermon on the Mount. As I pondered the directives that Christ gave to his followers, I selected the one that I felt I had the greatest difficulty with:

> But I say unto you, love your enemies, bless them that curse you, do good to them that hate you. For if you forgive men their trespasses, your Heavenly Father will also forgive you. But if you forgive not men their trespasses, neither will your Father forgive your trespasses.

As I meditated on this passage, I knew how many times I had violated the Lord's teaching. Right now, I had to admit, I was nursing a counter-hate within me for those who had hurt me and my loved ones.

I knew I had to forgive those who abused me. And if I couldn't do it by myself, then I would ask Christ to do it through me, giving me the strength and power to not only forgive those who hated me, but yes, even to love them as our Savior commanded.

Father, perhaps I can forgive, I pleaded, *but how can I love them?*

It seemed impossible.

And then, one of my attackers, a former friend who had sharply assailed me, came to my office some months later pleading for help. His daughter was in difficulty and he was desperate. As I saw the pain in his eyes my heart went out to him, and I took his trembling hand in mine. I understood his grief as only another father could. I was able to help his daughter and our friendship was restored, stronger than ever.

Through this I began to see my "enemies" in Christ's light as friends, acquaintances, fellow lawyers, sinners as was I, blinded by misunderstanding. After all, Christ had forgiven my many sins; who was I not to forgive others.

Though it did not transpire overnight, and I had many second thoughts, I was finally able to forgive and even love them with the Lord's help. A heavy weight seemed to lift from my shoulders, and I was able to carry on my work in a more relaxed manner.

Hate between men can be terribly strong, enough to change the course of history. But far more powerful is God's love as taught by his church. Hitler, I believe, recognized this. And thus he took every means at his command to weaken the church in Germany. Enough good men and women forsook the church and Christ's teachings and joined the forces of hate, which ultimately destroyed them.

But in Mississippi and Washington, D.C., good finally overcame evil.

Tension had ebbed at Ole Miss. Meredith was continuing to attend there and was even beginning to have friendly conversations with some of his fellow students. But the charges filed by the Department of Justice against Governor Barnett still stood. His conduct had been in willful disregard and in defiance of the restraining orders issued by the court. His acts, read the charges, had encouraged law-enforcement officials and others in Mississippi to obstruct and prevent the entry of Meredith onto the university campus.

There were still pretrial hearings and court rulings to be made before the case could come to court. One of these was to be before the Supreme Court. On the morning the case was to be heard, I appeared at the Justice Department in a business suit. I was at a desk checking over some papers when I heard an exclamation. I looked up to see Archibald Cox, the solicitor general, staring at my suit.

"Leon," he gasped, "you can't go into court like that. You're representing the government. You have to wear a morning coat and tails."

"I don't have any," I said. Formal attire had never appealed to me. However, Cox insisted and borrowed a cutaway from a member of his staff. Unfortunately the man weighed forty pounds less than I did, and I felt like a penguin stuffed into a shrunken tuxedo. All during my argument before the court, I was worried that the seams would split, especially when I sat down.

But both the borrowed cutaway and our position in this instance held up.

However, in the end the government suit against Barnett was dismissed. Two-and a-half years had passed since the ordeal at the University of Mississippi. His term as governor had ended and conditions had changed at the university. A majority of the justices believed that the changed conditions had brought about full compliance with the court's orders, that Barnett had, in effect, purged himself, and the charges could be dismissed.

And so it was done.

The result was interesting in one way. Though the dismissal was widely publicized, I did not receive one letter of complaint or approval. Neither did Nick Katzenbach who by then had succeeded Robert Kennedy as attorney general. The angry threats and criticism that had deafened me when I was preparing to prosecute Barnett had no echo when the calm operation of our system of justice let him off.

I also learned that such attitudes of condemnation did not last long. In later days the very individuals who were loudest in their criticism and severest in their verbal attacks were among the first to seek my counsel and help when trouble faced them.

Today the Ole Miss campus is quiet. Civil rights have come a long way since those days. As I look back on the inflammatory time when a governor used the police powers of his state to escalate his battle with the federal government, I shudder to think how close we were to the gravest conflict between federal and state authority since the Civil War.

But the poison of civil confrontations did not die in the streetcars and schools of the South; it exploded again in the late 1960s when the college campuses became alive with the fire of civil disobedience. I served on the National Commission on the Causes and Prevention of Violence for President Lyndon Johnson. After many months of listening to enlightened individuals, research, and study, a majority of the commission concluded:

> For several years, our youth has been exposed to dramatic demonstrations of disdain for law by persons for whom exemplary conduct was to be expected. Segregationist governors had disobeyed court orders and had proclaimed their defiance of judicial institutions; civil rights leaders had openly disobeyed court injunctions and had urged their followers to do likewise; striking teachers' union members had contemptuously ignored judicial decrees. It was not surprising that college students, following adult example, destroyed scientific equipment and research data, interfered with rights of others by occupying laboratories and classrooms, and in several instances temporarily closed their colleges.

But such disorder did not end in the 60s. Even now, policemen, firemen, teachers, and other public employees in various cities have gone on strike despite laws against it.

Where the right to strike is not forbidden by law and is conducted in an orderly fashion, society respects that right.

But recently in one of our larger cities striking firemen watched an entire block of buildings burn down without attempting to control the fire, which threatened a major portion of the community.

In another metropolis, striking teachers formed picket lines around schools when children were reporting for classes. As I watched on television, I was dismayed to see large groups of teachers—who were obliged to instill in these highly impressionable young people concepts of good citizenship—screaming, swearing, and jeering. Some were arrested, sentenced for contempt of court, and jailed. I wondered if they realized the principles they were teaching their students to emulate.

What is even more difficult for me to understand is the police officer, who has taken an oath to uphold the law, deliberately breaking it by striking and then disregarding a court order directing his return to duty.

In view of this can children be expected to respect the law?

I am completely sympathetic to the poor working conditions and inadequate salaries that some policemen, firemen, and teachers have to endure. For years I have been advocating that these people so vital to society's maintenance enjoy adequate compensation and good working conditions. But they must remember that the open forum of the city council, the state legislatures, and the polls are available to them as proper resorts for remedial action.

As I think back on the 1960s when hate had momentarily replaced love, I recall a book a friend gave me entitled *Love, Beauty and Harmony in Sufism*.

I had not heard of Sufism before, and as I leafed through the book I became interested in some of the passages. Sufism, I learned, consisted of the philosophies and ideologies of the Persians. Some of the most beautiful poetry ever written was penned by Persians based on Sufism's tenets.

The volume pointed out that Sufi poets were: "idolized by Persians because their life and work embody the human moral conscience in its purest and most persuasive state. It was said that their concern for the freedom of ideas, their hatred of cruelty, their fight against hypocrisy and religious persecution, their opposition to injustice and inequities were qualities that endeared them both to their contemporaries and to posterity."

The Sufi movement was born in the tenth century as a protest against the tyranny and corruption of an oppressive and materialistic society. It represented the antithesis of intolerance and inhumanity.

Today, this same nation, Persia, is called Iran. And we

know how strife-torn, stricken with rebellion, and enmeshed in terror it is. As this is written, Iran is in the grip of a religious leader whose cruel acts and flagrant breaches of international law are unparalleled in modern times. We will never know how many hundreds of its people have been dragged into the executioner's yard to be shot.

What went wrong? How did the pure thoughts expressed by their poets in gems of rhetoric become shunted aside to be replaced by godless deeds and holocaustal violence?

It can happen anywhere, I believe. I had seen similar fruits in another nation famous for its fine composers and poets. And it can happen in our own country if we allow hatred and intolerance to divide us, if we do not follow the precepts of love and compassion as taught us by Jesus Christ.

There is enough pain and sorrow in this world without our adding to it. I was to be reminded of this in a most tragic way. For I was about to enter my own personal odyssey of grief from which I could not seem to recover.

15
Swamp Fox

A soft summer breeze rippled the fields of the Circle J ranch on that July morning in 1972. My grandson Mike, now a young man, had risen early to see Jeannette and me off to a convention of the State Bar of Texas in Houston, where as president of the American Bar Association, I was to speak. Mike's plans for the day were to cut down some dead timber out in the far reaches of the ranch and saw it up. Then, since some of his friends from Duke University would visit him in a few days, he wanted to check out an eating place he felt they might enjoy.

We walked to my car, his arm around me as we discussed plans for entertaining his friends. We said good-bye, and as I drove toward the gate I could see him in my rearview mirror, waving and then turning toward his jeep.

That evening I pursued with interest some of the news

articles that had followed the June 17 arrest of five men who'd broken into the Watergate headquarters of the Democratic National Committee in Washington. Evidently one of the burglars worked for the Committee for the Reelection of the President. Subsequent headlines linked more and more committee and White House personnel to the Watergate burglary and other espionage and sabotage on behalf Richard Nixon's reelection campaign. It seemed a strange business, and the stories made me uneasy about what was happening in Washington.

The next morning I was at an early breakfast meeting at the Shamrock Hilton when a friend, Robert Calvert, former chief justice of the Texas Supreme Court, stepped up and simply said, "Come with me."

Wondering what he had on his mind, I followed him, speaking to friends and acquaintances as we passed among the tables. He led me out of the front door of the hotel to the sidewalk where I found my daughter, Joanie, waiting at a car. Her face was strained and pale.

"Dad," she said quietly, "Mike is dead."

I stared at her in disbelief. Joanie explained what had happened as the car took us home.

After cutting and sawing wood the day I left, Mike had driven to the restaurant. He had found himself on strange roads since he hadn't been in that area before. His car hit loose gravel, swerved, and overturned. His skull had been crushed.

Blinded by tears and gripped by grief, I rode in silence, fighting the reality of Mike being gone. I simply could not accept the fact that I'd never see him again.

I went through the funeral service in a daze. Our minister, Jack Lancaster, was out of town and an assistant pastor officiated. But I have no memory of what was said. Instead my mind went back through the years, remembering the little boy I had known and loved.

Mike had become more and more of a son to my wife and me, because we had helped take care of him when he was a child. He had called Jeannette and me "Oma" and "Opa," pet names for grandma and grandpa in German, just as our children had called my mother and father.

Every hour I had been able to spare, Jeannette, little Mike, and I would head to the hill country. As a tyke, Mike loved to wear a cowboy hat and chaps. He "pertended" to be Roy Rogers and to him, I was Roy's "fodder." Together we had fought the Indians from one end of the ranch to the other—and never lost a battle.

One day the Houston *Chronicle* had carried this item:

> When the telephone operator in the law offices of Fulbright, Crooker, Freeman, Bates and Jaworski answered a call the other morning a childish treble asked for Mr. Jaworski. "You know, he works there," the voice offered helpfully.
>
> As it happened, Jaworski wasn't in at the moment but his secretary took the message and left a memo. The call was from Jaworski's 5-year-old grandson, Mike.
>
> When Jaworski got back to the office there was a stack of memos waiting for him: "Call Mr. Silverspoon about the bank merger"; "Call Mr. Gotrocks, he's being sued for $1,000,000"; "Call Mrs. Heavydough about her income tax"; etc. etc. Those weren't exactly what the memos said but they all related to Big Business. Except one—the one on the top of the stack, and the one Jaworski answered first:
>
> Call Mike—he wants to talk with you about the Indians.

Of course I called him back first.

At the ranch we'd explore the densely wooded lands of spreading live oaks, Spanish oaks, elm, and wild cherry trees, and pick our way through the cedar brakes on adventures in which I began to feel like a boy again.

On many occasions we buried "treasures," trinkets he had assembled. The metal coffee-can containers would be buried in the most remote reaches of the ranch, which I hardly even knew existed, and soon forgot. When we'd look for them a year later, Mike knew precisely where each one was buried.

On one hot afternoon, returning from an exploratory journey, Mike and I trudged toward the ranch house, both of us looking forward to some of Jeannette's cold lemonade.

As we walked on toward the house, which was now about two-hundred yards away, I could hear his breath coming in short gasps. Sometimes I would walk too fast, forgetting that his legs were much shorter than mine.

Suddenly, he piped, "Opa, look."

I stopped and turned. He was pointing to a tree that, partially uprooted in some long-ago storm, had continued to grow parallel to the ground. It offered a perfect resting spot and we walked over to it. There was something unusual about the surroundings. Several huge cedar bushes had clustered around the sideways tree and a giant oak towered over it, all forming a charming little grove.

For several minutes we sat there, Mike's boots dangling from the gnarled tree trunk. Neither of us said anything, just listened to the soft whisper of the breeze sighing through the cedars and the distant call of a crow from some field.

Mike lifted his face to me, "I *like* this place, Opa."

From then on the little grove became our sanctuary.

As we returned from exploration, Indian battle, or simply cutting firewood, it became a tradition for us to pause there. One day when I rose to continue on to the house, Mike said, "You go on, Opa. I want to stay here for a while."

"OK, Mike," I said, looking at him. "I'll tell Oma you'll be along shortly."

When Jeannette asked about my sidekick, I laughed. "Don't know what he's doing out there. Maybe he's meditating."

Ten minutes later when he had finally come in and was drinking his lemonade, I asked what had kept him so long. He looked at me through big eyes, "Talking with Swamp Fox."

From then on he always made it a point to halt there alone "to talk with Swamp Fox."

For years I did not know who Swamp Fox was. But I speculated that he was a character Mike had read about; for he learned to read at an early age and consumed every book he could get his hands on. Now I know that Francis Marion, an

American general in the Revolutionary War, won the nickname Swamp Fox for his daring raids.

Mike's openness and honesty was another trait that became obvious when he was quite young. He frequently accompanied us to restaurants. On one occasion Jeannette's steak turned out to be more than she could handle.

"It's so good, Leon, I hate to waste it," she had said.

In those days it was not customary to take part of one's meal home unless it was scraps for the dog.

She beckoned to the girl and said, "Would you please wrap up this meat? I would like to take it home to the dog."

Before the waitress could answer, Mike piped up, wide-eyed, "Oma, I didn't know you had a dog."

He was not being impudent. He loved his grandmother. But in his untarnished mind he could see no reason for not forthrightly asking for a bag. Jeannette had blushed and laughed, but we both got the point.

In the following years we frequently took leftovers home, but never "for the dog."

Years went by, and Mike began calling me "colonel" as the older members of our family did. I stayed young with Mike, passing him a football as he'd streak across the lawn, cheering him on in swimming contests, and attending sports events with him. His cousins loved him, too, and Jeannette and I would enjoy watching the five of them splash and play games in the ranch pool.

Brilliant in history and English literature, Mike became a champion debater in high school, a fact, which of course, warmed my heart. He was frequently chosen by fellow students to represent his class. The faculty must have had confidence in him, too, as he was often called upon to deal with matters of mutual concern to faculty and students. When in his late teens he said he wanted to become a lawyer, I couldn't have been prouder.

Mike graduated from high school in 1971. He had applied to five different colleges for prelaw studies, and I worried a little because each was among those most difficult to enter.

However he was accepted by all five and settled on Duke University.

When he left for college, I said, "Mike, now you call me if at any time you need help." I knew how it was with beginning students: there were always some unforeseen expenses.

A week later he called. Before I could speak, he said quickly, "Colonel, I'm not in need of any help." There was silence for a moment, then: "I just wanted to visit with you." We had a great time talking about the fun we had had the past summer.

He was especially proud of my becoming president-elect of the American Bar Association. The ABA is a national organization with a voluntary membership of some two-hundred-sixty-thousand lawyers and is recognized as the spokesman of the profession. I was then spending about half of my time addressing state bar meetings and local bar associations around the country.

"Don't get too busy," he said, "so that we don't have any time together come summer."

Mike did very well in his first year of college. He had returned in the summer of 1972 enthused over resuming our work together on the ranch. By now he was almost a man, six feet tall, handsomely blond, well built. But the summer had shot by like an arrow. He was making plans to return to Duke in August to begin his sophomore year.

One afternoon we were driving back to the house in the jeep when we passed the little grove we had first discovered so many years ago.

As I saw it I said, "By the way, Mike, what is the name of the fellow you used to visit down there?"

Flashing his white teeth in a grin, he gave me a playful poke. "Aw, c'mon, colonel, you darn well know the name of that fellow."

The organ music swelled in the First Presbyterian Church, and I was pulled from my reverie to the somber reality of a funeral, a memorial service for this beloved boy. I walked from the church trying to be pleasant to those around me, but still lost in thoughts of our times together.

Weeks went by before I finally accepted the fact that Mike was gone. And then I was even more distraught. There were no words, nothing that could comfort me. Memories of the loss of my brother, Joe, crushed in on me. He was another fine young man, the apple of my father's eye with a promising career ahead of him. I remembered how my heartbroken father had wept over his loss in times alone, yet still bore up bravely to others.

"It is God's will," he had said, his voice quaking. "We must accept it."

I had tried to understand then, and I attempted to understand now. But try as I might I could find nothing in my father's words or conduct that would lessen my almost uncontrollable bereavement. I remembered the elderly lawyer who on hearing of my brother's death had said he could never understand why the Lord let so many rascals run loose and then took a fine young man like Joe.

There was nothing anyone could say or do that would help me understand the violent snuffing out of Mike's life, Mike who had so much to give.

When our minister returned to Houston he called and wanted to talk with me. Even though Jack Lancaster was a dear friend on whom I would be quick to rely for support, I found myself freezing inside. I did not want promises of hope, of life continuing, of God's will. It had all become meaningless.

"No, Jack," I said emotionlessly, "it will have to wait awhile."

When next Jeannette and I returned to the ranch, I did not enjoy it anymore. I seemed to walk in a daze, doing things automatically.

"The chain saw and the tools," I found myself saying. "I'll have to find where he left them." Jeannette went along in the jeep. Our search was much longer then we had expected when Jeannette finally spotted the tools on the side of a hill. I picked them up and put them into the back of the jeep.

As I drove back to the ranch house, we passed near the little grove that Mike and I had discovered many years ago, the place where he used to talk to Swamp Fox.

I glanced in the other direction.

Swamp Fox had lost his meaning.

The little boy was gone.

The wonder and delight had vanished like morning hill mist.

I did not want to be reminded of lost dreams anymore.

16

The Nation
at the Crossroads

It was Sunday morning early in November, 1973. Services had just ended in the First Presbyterian Church in Houston when my pastor, Jack Lancaster, came up and asked if my family and I would accompany him to the chapel.

Not quite sure of what he had in mind, we dutifully followed him to the attractive little, white-walled Georgian-style chapel. There I was surprised to find over twenty-five people assembled, including the two associate pastors and all the church elders.

"Since you'll be going to Washington this week, we want to pray for you," said Dr. Lancaster. It wasn't the capital city that my friends were concerned about; it was the Watergate trial. The seemingly minor burglary in June of 1972 had blown up into a national scandal and a veritable maze of accusations and denials. A Senate Watergate Committee had been formed, and began holding nationally televised hearings in May. Appearing before the committee in June, John Dean, former counsel to President Richard Nixon, had accused Nixon himself of involvement in the Watergate break-in and cover-up.

It was difficult to know where truth lay, or what the proper judicial and constitutional procedures for getting at the truth should be. The trial was a real meat grinder that had already chewed up some good people. And I was soon to leave Houston to take over as the special Watergate prosecutor.

I was deeply moved by my friends' concern. As we sat in the front pew one by one the elders and ministers seated in various rows behind us prayed for God's guidance and strength for me and my family as I fulfilled my responsibilities in Washington.

". . . Lord, guide Leon's thoughts, words, and deeds through your Holy Spirit. . . ." Their different prayers rang out fervently, and I joined their supplications, knowing that without the Lord's help I would be completely lost.

These prayers and the continued prayers and calls to Washington once I was gone were an important contribution to my role in Watergate. I had first been contacted about the post some time before this.

One afternoon in late October my secretary said, "General Alexander Haig is on the line."

I knew that he had become President Nixon's chief of staff after H.R. Haldeman had resigned back in April.

His voice had been calm and measured. "Mr. Jaworski, we are gravely concerned. Would you come to Washington to talk about serving as the special Watergate prosecutor?"

"I'm sorry," I had answered, thanking him for the thought, "but I have already looked at it once. I just don't believe the office has enough independence," I added, remembering the infamous "Saturday Night Massacre," on October 20, in which the former special prosecutor, Archibald Cox, was fired. Attempting to untangle the confusing evidence, Cox had subpoenaed nine tape recordings of presidential conversations—and had been fighting for them unsuccessfully ever since July. On October 19, he was ordered not to seek any more tapes. Instead of complying he had revealed the ultimatum to the press the next day and was fired that evening.

"It's a completely different situation now," Haig urged. "You can have all the independence you want."

"Well, Archie Cox thought he had independence, but he was axed by the president."

"I can assure you; you will have real independence."

Still I had demurred.

"Well, Mr. Jaworski, could you at least come up here and talk?"

After a moment's thought, I said that I would.

"All right, I'm sending a plane for you in the morning."

The next day a small U.S. Air Force plane had picked me up at the Ellington Air Force Base outside of Houston. As the plane with its seven uniformed crew members and one passenger, myself, jetted across the continent, I reminisced about my friend Lyndon Johnson who had died early that year. How often, I thought, I had flown to Washington at his request in earlier years. Now another president was bringing me here.

I mused about the man who appeared to be at the center of this controversy. Through the years I had been impressed by Nixon's resoluteness and ability. I had voted for him in 1968 and again in 1972. I had also been impressed by his Quaker heritage, for I had long admired these "Seekers of Truth," noted for their forthright honesty. I just couldn't believe that this man would have buried himself in the actions of deception some newspapermen and investigators suspected.

When we landed at Andrews Air Force Base in Washington, a car had been waiting to whisk me to the White House where I was met by the handsome, blue-eyed Haig who, even in civilian clothes, looked like a general.

After preliminary conversation, his soft voice became grave. "I'm putting the patriotic monkey on your back, Mr. Jaworski. The situation in this country is almost revolutionary. Things are about to come apart."

He had leaned forward in his chair. "The only hope of stabilizing the situation is for the president to announce that someone in whom the country has confidence has agreed to serve as special prosecutor."

I told him there just wasn't a strong enough guarantee that I could operate without interference.

He offered me assurance from the president that he was giving me complete independence and the further stipulation that he would not discharge me, except for extraordinary improprieties, without first getting approval from the leadership of both parties in the House and the Senate, plus the House and Senate Judiciary Committees.

To help convince me that I should accept the post, he brought in acting General Bork, Attorney General designate Saxbe, plus White House lawyers Fred Buzhardt and Leonard Gament and presidential advisers Melvin Laird and Bryce Harlow.

When we were finally alone again, I breathed a silent prayer and reexamined my conscience. For years I had been exhorting law students and fellow lawyers not to shun unpopular cases. How could I do so now?

For a moment I sat there in silence. What would God have of me? Could turning my back on this terrifying problem possibly be his will?

I looked up at Haig. "I accept," I said quietly.

He seemed delighted. "We'll announce it immediately. Remember," he added, "the key words in this news conference are to be that you have the right to take the president to court."

"I'll remember," I said, knowing that there might be moments in the future when those words would be my only security.

That evening I had returned to Houston to be met by an avalanche of newsmen and press photographers. They had surrounded our house, and at five o'clock the next morning were knocking at our door again.

As they barraged me with questions I began to get the

nagging feeling that many people felt Nixon and his entourage had selected me as a safe, upper-middle-class bet. As some wag later suggested: "After all, doesn't he comb his white hair just like Archie Bunker?"

I had a long-standing engagement that day to be grand marshal of the Baylor University homecoming parade, so I went to Waco, where not only the press but friends and acquaintances besieged me.

"Leon, you're sticking your head in a buzz saw," warned one lawyer friend.

Others chided me for taking the post.

"How can you go against such a fine man as Richard Nixon?" questioned a matron with tears in her eyes. I assured her that I was not entering the endeavor with the idea of going against anyone, that my effort would be to seek the truth.

My remaining days in Houston had flown by and on that last Sunday in church with my family, I thanked the elders and Pastor Jack for their prayers, and asked them to please continue praying for me.

Deep in my heart I knew I would be needing their prayers desperately.

The next day my plane landed at Washington's Dulles Airport where another crowd of press people met me, and I was driven to a building in northwest Washington at 1425 K Street, which housed my offices. Security was tight, armed guards checked us, and television surveillance followed every move. When I was ushered into my office, the security officer asked me to keep the window blinds closed at all times.

"Why?" I asked.

"So someone with a telescope in another building can't read anything on your desk," he replied.

Nothing was on my desk so I pulled back a blind and looked out. Across Vermont Avenue I saw a low, old building. I recognized it. I had lived on its third floor when I had attended George Washington University fifty years ago. We had both aged a lot since then.

I was introduced to my staff of some twenty-five people and was amazed at how very young they were. Most appeared to be in their late twenties or early thirties. I also realized they may have been thinking, "How old he is!" But they all seemed like sharp, intelligent people.

Finally when my door was closed and I sat in my office alone, I again prayed that the Lord would be with me, guiding and sustaining me so that I could fulfill the responsibilities that I had been sworn in to discharge. All my law education, experience, and background would not be enough in this situation as I was very soon to find out.

Everything exploded one unforgettable day in December, 1973.

A number of White House tapes had been delivered to us; they had come to us at my request and some had been extricated from the White House through a court proceeding instituted by my predecessor, Archibald Cox.

On that mid-December afternoon, Carl Feldbaum, whose duty it was to preview these tapes, beckoned me into his office, handed me a set of earphones, and said I should hear one particular tape right away. It was a recording of a conversation on March 21, 1973, between President Nixon, his chief of staff, Bob Haldeman, and counsel, John Dean.

As I listened to the voices I was dumbfounded.

The president of the United States, the number-one law enforcement officer of our nation, was conspiring with two top aides to obstruct justice and commit at least two, maybe more, serious felonies!

I removed the headset, trying hard not to reveal my emotions as Carl Feldbaum and another assistant sat watching me.

"Er, ah, I didn't catch a part of that very clearly," I said, adjusting the headset. "Let's hear it again." I barely listened to the replay, but it gave me time to think of what I should say to my men.

"Thanks, Carl," I said, matter-of-factly. "If you run across anything else in this tape or the others, give me a call."

Endeavoring to be casual, I strolled to my office and closed the door, asking my secretary to hold all calls for a while. "I'm falling behind in my work," I explained.

As I sat at my desk studying the wall, scenes flashed before me like pictures in a slide show.

Nixon giving his First Inaugural Address in 1969, memorable words that had thrilled me and millions of Americans: "Our crisis today is in reverse. We find ourselves rich in goods, but ragged in spirit; reaching with magnificent precision for the moon, but falling into raucous discord on earth.

"To a crisis of the spirit, we need an answer of the spirit," he charged. "And to find that answer, we need only look within ourselves."

Could this be the same man who had sat with his two henchmen on March 21, plotting a way to keep Haldeman and other White House officials from having to testify about their involvement in the Watergate activities?

In my mind I pictured the White House, now only a few miles from my office: its snow-white pillars, which most Americans identified with justice and authority, and the stark white Oval Office of the president of the United States. Nixon had sat at the chief executive's massive, carved mahogany desk, flanked by the American and the District of Columbia flags and conspired with Dean and Haldeman to evade the law like criminals in a dingy saloon.

Their voices as they discussed the possibility of testifying before the Senate Watergate Committee echoed in my mind:

"You can take the Fifth Amendment," Dean had asserted.

"That's right. That's right," said President Nixon.

"You can say you forgot, too, can't you?" broke in Haldeman.

"That's right," repeated Nixon.

"But you can . . ." broke in Dean worriedly. "You're in a very high risk perjury situation!"

"That's right!" snapped Nixon. "Just be ------ sure you say, 'I don't remember. I can't recall. I can't give any honest' . . ."

As his voice echoed in my memory repeating over and over: "I don't remember. I can't recall," I remembered Nixon's speech to the nation on April 30, 1973, when the ugly head of Watergate had just begun to surface. "This office is a sacred trust, and I am determined to be worthy of that trust . . ."

In speaking of the excesses in political campaigns he had said: "The lesson is clear. America in its political campaigns must not again fall into the trap of letting the end, however great that end is, justify the means."

A chill came over me. In his own words Nixon had outlined the web in which he and his staff had become enmeshed, a web I had seen another country caught in: the single-minded pursuit of "national interest," which brushes aside any questions of the morality of means in achieving that goal.

My mind went back to the tapes I had just heard and a conversation between John Dean and President Richard Nixon on that same day, discussing the blackmail money needed to maintain the Watergate cover-up.

"Now, where, where are the soft spots on this?" asked John Dean. "Well, first of all there's the, there's the problem of this continued blackmail . . ."

"Right," interrupted the president.

". . . which will not go on now," continued Dean, "it'll go on when these people are in prison, and it will compound the obstruction of justice situation. It'll cost money. It's dangerous. Nobody, nothing—people around here are not pros at this sort of thing. This is the sort of thing Mafia people can do: washing money, getting clean money, and things like that. Uh, we're . . . we just don't know about those things because we're not used to, you know, we are not criminals and not used to dealing in that business. It's uh, it's un . . ."

"Plus there's a real problem in raising money. Uh, Mitchell has been working on raising some money. . . ," Dean informed President Nixon.

"How much money do you need?" asked the president.

"I would say these people are going to cost, uh, a million dollars over the next, uh, two years."

"We could get that."

"Uh, huh."

". . . What I mean is," I could visualize Nixon leaning forward, "you could, you could get a million dollars. And you could get it in cash. I, I know where it could be gotten."

Five months after this conversation with Dean, the president said in a written statement to the nation on August 15, 1973: "It was on March 21 (the day that these tapes had been made) that I learned of some of the activities upon which charges of the cover-up are now based. I was told then that funds had been raised for payments to the defendants. . . . But I was only told that the money had been used for attorney's fees and family support, not that it had been paid to procure silence from the recipients."

The tapes I had just heard were a direct contradiction to what he had told the American people.

In his speech accompanying this written statement, he had again referred to what I felt was the heart of the matter. "As we look at Watergate in the longer perspective, we can see that its abuses resulted from the assumption by those involved that their cause placed them beyond the reach of these rules that apply to other persons and hold a free society together."

Now I knew how deep and far-reaching the Watergate investigation would be. I also knew how traumatic it would be for the nation, and for the president and his staff. I shuddered, and for a moment wished desperately that I had never been asked to take on this assignment.

I drew in a deep breath. There was work to be done. The question was: where to start?

Two of my assistants knew what I knew; other staff members would learn of it. But no one knew what interpretation I would give this evidence, or what my course of action would be.

17
A Deepening Quagmire

The murmur of office activity outside my door quieted, and I realized it was after hours. But it may as well have been 5:30 A.M. for all I knew, as I was lost in a mire of swirling thoughts. I was facing probably the most difficult crossroad of my life.

The person I contemplated prosecuting was the leader of the greatest nation on earth, just returned to office with a 62½ percent majority vote. Trouble brewed in the Middle East. Russia still loomed ominously, and the wounds of Vietnam were fresh. I remembered how Alexander Haig had dropped pungent comments about unsettled foreign affairs as I had pleaded for more cooperation from the White House in furnishing records and tapes.

I knew my first obligation was to take the tape I had just listened to, along with others, to the grand jury. Then what?

The final decision would be mine and mine alone. The grand jury could not indict the president without my approval. My staff could take no action without it. No judge could tell me what to do in this situation.

But could a president in office be indicted for an obstruction of justice? I knew that if a president had committed something as serious as murder there would be little question, but in this case I wasn't quite sure. To complicate matters further, there was the House committee considering Articles of Impeachment. Would the judicial process permit a president to be exposed to a criminal proceeding while facing impeachment charges?

For days we searched through law books finding no answers. There was no precedent, and any comparisons were simply too scant or remote.

In my experience in private litigation as well as in public service, I had always believed that there was no problem, no matter how complex or uncertain, that did not have a solution. But here was a new one, of much greater dimension than any other.

I was facing a legal obstacle course of unprecedented complications. It would have to be navigated through a series of moves for which I would be solely responsible. I must not make a mistake.

I could not entrust my dilemma to outsiders—not to anyone. I could not even indicate a leaning, lest my staff, already rife with speculation, misinterpret my action.

After carefully thinking over the matter and praying for guidance, I reached a decision and made my first move.

It was just before Christmas when I called Alexander Haig to tell him that I needed to visit him before returning to Houston for a brief holiday.

We met in the White House Map Room, which Franklin Roosevelt had used in World War II to study the ongoing action. As a waiter brought us coffee and tea we sat down, and I came right to the point.

I told Haig that I feared Richard Nixon had committed a criminal offense, and gave him the reasons.

Haig admitted that the March 21 tape was terrible indeed.

But he said that White House lawyers had told him there was no criminal offense involved as far as the president was concerned.

"I can't agree, Al. Based on what I heard—and what we already knew—I'm afraid the president engaged in criminal conduct."

We went back and forth, discussing whether I or the White House lawyers were right.

Finally, I said, "Al, I want to tell you something. I think you should get the finest criminal lawyer you can find—someone not connected with the White House in any way—and let him study the tapes."

I can't begin to tell you how much I regret this and how concerned I am," I told Haig, promising to talk with him as soon as I returned to Washington.

Haig's usual ramrod-straight posture had slumped; I could see that he was visibly shaken. He slowly shook his head, "This is not what the lawyers say."

We walked from the Map Room to the diplomatic entrance. Snow had blanketed the White House grounds. As my car was brought to the door Haig was silent, thoughtful.

"It's important, Al," I said. "Get that lawyer, the best you can find."

Tears glistened in his blue eyes as we shook hands and I turned to my car. I, too, felt terrible. I wished him a Merry Christmas, adding how much I regretted our meeting under such circumstances.

Later, as my plane headed into a setting sun, I tried to concentrate on the upcoming Christmas celebration with my family. But I couldn't escape the realization that the Watergate hornet's nest was buzzing louder and louder. No matter how much I tried to do the right thing, I would certainly suffer the stings.

Christmas-tree lights twinkled invitingly in the windows of our Houston home, and I looked forward to a relaxing few days. But I had hardly stepped into the door when the telephone rang. It was General Haig telling me that he had followed my advice and contacted some attorneys. They had stated that Nixon had not committed a criminal act. He gave me a technical explanation of what they had said.

"I'm sorry, Al," I replied. "I cannot agree. I've given the matter very careful consideration and have come to a different conclusion. . . . What attorneys have you consulted?"

He said he had talked with two lawyers on the White House staff in whom he had confidence.

"But, Al, they have both been identified with advising Nixon and are in a poor position to judge the nature of his acts from a legal standpoint. They are both clearly biased." I again urged him to obtain outside counsel.

As I hung up the phone I realized that there was just so much one could do. I went into the kitchen to see what Jeannette was baking for Christmas.

It was great to be back home and, of course, at our first opportunity we headed for the ranch. There I put my chain saw and other tools in the back of the jeep and drove into the hills. This time I did not detour around the little grove where Swamp Fox lived. In fact, I drove straight to it, got out of the jeep, and walked over to the tree trunk and sat down.

A cold, brisk wind blew off the hills but for some reason I felt strangely comfortable. Perhaps it was the cedars breaking the wind, but I found it pleasant to sit here and reminisce.

My healing from the pain of Mike's death had probably started right here in the hills a little while after his funeral. David Draper, my daughter Claire's oldest boy who was sixteen, had come with me to finish the wood cutting Mike had started. Mike had felled a large dead oak, and David and I prepared to cut it up. I had not really wanted to come here at that time; a bitterness over Mike's death still filled me. But somehow I felt a strange pulling toward this place.

David, tall for his age with black hair and lively brown eyes, waited for me to give him directions. I studied the oak for a moment, and then told him where we'd begin cutting.

"We must do this real well," I said, "because Mike is watching us."

That moment was the beginning of my embracing the reminders of Mike, not as sad pangs, but as blessed memories, which strengthened and comforted me.

Many years before when Jeannette and I were at Williamsburg, Virginia, we had visited a blacksmith shop where the smithy made small horseshoes with individuals' names hammered into them. We had bought four, each bearing the name of a grandson, and I had nailed them in a horseshoe circle onto the door of my toolhouse at the ranch.

Once I had been able to return to this glade, I had taken Mike's horseshoe from the door and nailed it to the tree trunk he sat on as he visited with Swamp Fox. Here, too, I had replanted a young elm that had originally grown on the banks of Geronimo Creek where I had played as a small boy.

Now, on this gray December day, I sat back on the benchlike tree trunk and looked up into the sky. The sun suddenly broke out of the overcast for a moment, like the quick smile Mike would flash, and somehow I felt his presence. I wondered what young men like him would think of Watergate.

I thought of the many conversations Mike and I had had about the student unrest of the 1960s. Mike had had an unusually clear grasp of political and economic problems, and when I would express my consternation at student disenchantment, he would reply, "Well, colonel, you've got to understand the basis for their cynicism about some public officials." He then went on to enumerate flagrant examples of dishonesty.

"But," I had often countered, "should an entire institution of government become suspect because of the corrupt practices of a few? The good and faithful officials rendering dedicated service deserve a better fate than to be so demeaned."

Now I knew our young people had reason to be disillusioned.

But corruption in office is no excuse for violence, in the 1960s or today. Under our democratic form of government, the individual can go to city hall, to the legislative chambers, and to a court of law. If enough citizens feel equally wronged, all can join in bringing about changes in our national constitution.

Such a move is not simple to make. But it shouldn't be simple. If it were, changes could easily result from temporary disenchantments or emotional reactions. A slow process assures careful and judicious handling along with a deep certainty that change is really needed.

In the difficult days ahead I knew I would have to work in this same manner. Slowly. Carefully. Always adhering to the laws of our land.

I returned to the ranch house renewed, happy for the opportunity to relax in the solitude of this grove that was now a memorial to my grandson's life.

That Christmas week with my jeep and saws I passed many of the spots where Mike and I had worked. I enjoyed reliving all the memories: the laughter over things that struck us as funny, the satisfaction in uprooting a large stump, the serious times we talked about his future.

I thanked God for those blessed memories, which would go on to enrich my life. And, instead of questioning God, I again came to appreciate him as the all-loving, all-knowing Father, whose plans we may now view through a glass darkly, but will someday see bright and clear.

During that week David went out with me often to pick up firewood, bring it back, and stack it by the various buildings. He was a sturdy lad and enjoyed outside work and learning to use the chain saw. We cut a path for a new cross fence and moved and stacked the tree trunks and limbs, which David later cut into chunks. He spent hours at this task, taking great pride in doing a beautiful job. It was a tonic to be with him. I needed his optimism and sparkling sense of humor to escape the foreboding presence of Watergate, which all too soon forced me back to Washington and the quagmire that awaited me there.

18
The Mounting Crisis

By early January, it became quite clear that President Nixon had decided to keep the facts buried. When I asked General Haig for more tapes, he suggested that I had received all the material I needed from the White House.

Each time we had extricated material from the White House before, Haig had tried to get an assurance from me that I would ask for nothing more.

"I can't determine what we will need until I have a chance to study what you've just given me," I would tell him. "Remember, we keep getting new information from individuals, which gives us reason to ask for more material."

Next, Haig cautioned me that the president was going to make all the decisions concerning our requests. "You probably won't receive any more tapes," he said.

"That would be a terrible mistake, Al. Congress won't like

it, and I don't believe the American people will."

"I realize that," Haig said, "but it's a calculated risk he's prepared to take."

By now, the House Judiciary Committee had assembled a staff and had appointed a chief counsel, John Doar, a very able lawyer and friend of mine. It seemed likely that Congress would give final authorization to the House impeachment inquiry in early February.

"This must be weighing heavily on the president's mind," I mentioned while meeting with General Haig.

"Well," he said, "everything he gives to you he'll have to give to the committee, won't he?"

We talked on in this vein; then I referred to the grand jurors' desire to have Nixon appear as a witness before them. As he had done in prior instances, Haig said the president would be willing to answer "written interrogatories" under oath.

Such testimony would have little value, I told Haig, because it seldom gives a full and accurate account of the facts. The answers can be prepared by lawyers and adopted by the witness. If the answers were unsatisfactory or incomplete, I could not pursue them as I could if oral testimony were given.

By this time it was clear that I was going to be in Washington for much longer than the few months I had earlier envisioned. I brought Jeannette back with me from one of my weekends at home. We set up housekeeping in a small apartment in the Jefferson Hotel, from which I was able to walk to work.

It wasn't long after this that we found ourselves attending services at the New York Avenue Presbyterian Church that cold, blustery morning of February 10, 1974, when the president and his party had joined the congregation.

The incriminating tapes were still fresh in my mind at that time, and I was feeling bitter about Nixon's hypocrisy. In those hours and hours of conversations in the White House, not once was there a reference to the glory of God. Not once was there a mention of seeking spiritual guidance through prayer. Even more pitiable, was the taking of God's name in vain, time after time. Why, I wondered, was there not just one simple prayer: "May we hold our honor sacred"?

And yet, I was beginning to recognize that I could not judge this man, that I could not continue on through this crucible in a spirit of vengeance. My staff and I would have to travel through the investigation purely in a search for truth so that right would prevail, not only for the people of the United States but for the president.

A month later the weather was balmy as March can sometimes be in Washington, and as I walked to work I enjoyed the crisp air and sunshine. But the Watergate investigation was still fraught with many complexities; we had no historical precedents to guide us. Moreover, the nation was strongly divided. A flood of letters came to me from citizens condemning Nixon, but these were matched by letters from those who warned about the serious consequences of interfering with the administration of our country. Many others condemned the news media for placing too much stress on Watergate developments.

I disagreed with this. I felt it was helpful to give the case as much coverage as possible. I hoped that the nation could see what I saw as the scene of events passed before them on television: one man reaching for power, assembling a group of ruthless henchmen around him, hiding their activities behind "executive privilege," and still believing that they were doing everything "for the good of the country."

I knew I had seen it all before. And, of course, I had: in the beginnings of the political party whose war crimes I had prosecuted.

I felt sure that the president didn't begin with ideas of eventual wrongdoing. But as time went by, he and his staff became callous, and laxity developed to where they did not differentiate between right and wrong.

My own course seemed clear to me. I would appear before the grand jury considering the Watergate burglary and the ensuing cover-up and recommend an indictment of John Mitchell, former attorney general, and the two top White

House aides, Bob Haldeman and John Ehrlichman, along with the others who participated in the Watergate cover-up.

I had decided against indicting Richard Nixon on the basis that the United States Supreme Court would probably not permit an indictment of an office-holding president on an obstruction-of-justice charge, grave as it was. Moreover, I was very concerned about the House Judiciary Committee's confronting Nixon and our indicting him at the same time. I felt certain that the Supreme Court would say that the government would have to decide on which course to follow: impeach him or bring him to trial—but not both.

Of course, once he was impeached, the president could be tried.

Now I was walking a tightrope. I knew that the White House wanted desperately for me to make a mistake, the kind that would tie things up in legal snarls for a long time. It was clear now that the White House was proceeding on a program of stonewalling and delay.

As I watched the desperate machinations of a group of men now determined to preserve their own skins, I couldn't help but be reminded of a sermon Jeannette and I had recently heard at the New York Avenue Presbyterian Church. Dr. J. Ernest Sommerville, pastor of the First Presbyterian Church in Philadelphia, was the visiting preacher, and his sermon topic was taken from Hebrews 11:10: "For he looked for a city which hath foundations, whose builder and maker is God."

"It was Abraham who was seeking such a city," said Dr. Sommerville, and he went on to portray its building blocks:

"Seek the Law.

"Seek the Word.

"Seek to do good.

"The old truth remains, you see, that you cannot achieve good by evil means. Apparently nothing is so difficult to understand in our present society. The tired old excuse is still that the end justifies the means. It has always been wrong. It is wrong still."

As I sat listening to him I could tell that this minister had seen the handwriting on the wall, and he was boldly talking about it, though Watergate had not fully peaked. Although he did not know all that I did, he knew enough to drive home the word from Holy Writ: there is no way that either a nation, a state, a community, a church, or an individual can blossom and flourish into greatness unless the foundations are in truth, righteousness, and justice.

Back in our office my staff members and I were very carefully preparing a report for the grand jury to transmit to Judge John J. Sirica at the time that the indictments of Mitchell, Haldeman, Ehrlichman, and others were to be returned. This secret report was directed to the House Judiciary Committee and was to be transmitted to it by the court.

I knew that this crucial report would be attacked. Transmitting evidence from a grand jury to another body, such as the House Judiciary Committee sitting in impeachment, had never been done before in our history.

The framing of this report was another crossroad. Should it indict Nixon or should it merely transmit facts that would speak for themselves?

Some of my aides favored designating evidence that proved Nixon guilty. After careful consideration, I felt this would be wrong. The facts would have to stand on their own—contain no accusations against him—or the report would not withstand the barrage of White House legal maneuvering. We would merely list every item of evidence that bore on Richard Nixon's conduct, gathered from tape recordings, documents, other evidence, and the testimony taken before the grand jury.

It would be a "road map," a step-by-step report of what happened in the Watergate cover-up.

The closing remarks of Nixon's Second Inaugural Speech—made only shortly before many of the devious machinations took place—rang through my mind as we followed the twisting, winding trail of cover-up attempts.

"We shall answer to God," he had said, "to history, and to our conscience for the way in which we use these years."

It was obvious from the road map that the beginning of his

second term as president would be very difficult to support before either God or man.

The White House strongly attacked the report, as I had expected, using Haldeman as the front man. But in the end the higher courts declared it a valid medium of transmission from one body of government to another. With the report in its hands, the House Judiciary Committee was able to summon witnesses, to consider evidence, and to begin taking positions on the Articles of Impeachment.

By now the extremists on both sides railed against me. Many people were clamoring for an indictment against Nixon. They claimed I wasn't pressing the prosecution strong enough. Some of their cries had the ring of frontier justice.

Others accused me of being too hard on the president, of being ruthlessly out to "get" him.

On top of this I was continuing to be stonewalled on every move by the tremendous power inherent in the White House.

I felt very much alone, knowing that I had to work within the slow, painstaking process of law to bring the president to justice. I could not discuss it publicly and kept quiet. And yet, in a way, I was not alone. For I believed I was supported by a host of others who also endeavored to work within the law in the government of this country.

It was during times like these that I was very grateful for a weekend respite back at the ranch. Such brief visits were made all the more enjoyable when my grandson, David, was able to be with me. As we worked together I quickly felt the cares of Watergate slipping away.

David had boundless energy, clearing brush and checking fences. We never failed to laugh about the time he had asked me to take him deer hunting. He had never hunted before, and on the way to the blind I gave him a crash course in the use of my rifle and the basic points of shooting, including the part of the deer to aim at.

Then in the backwoods I sat next to him in quiet suspense. When a large buck began entering a little clearing ahead of us, I had whispered to David: "Get set to squeeze the trigger as soon as you have him properly in sight."

Seconds that seemed like minutes passed and nothing happened.

I looked at David; his hands were trembling.

"Shoot, David!" I whispered.

"Colonel, I can't," he answered.

The deer, hearing our voices, jumped across the fence.

"Your last chance, David," I said.

He fired. We walked about thirty yards and found the buck, a clean shot.

David had turned to me, his face white. "Colonel, you'll never know how much I wished that buck had never shown up."

He was such a sensitive young man. He loved to play his guitar as we gathered with the family in the evening. He also liked to cook, and was quite good at it, delighting in trying new recipes in the ranch kitchen and discussing them with Jeannette. He was very close to his Aunt Joanie, who had taken a long time recovering from Mike's death. In a way, David began to fill in for Mike. When he wanted to confide in someone or seek counsel aside from his parents, he often went to her. It was good for both of them.

But the weekends like this were all too short, and when I returned to Washington it seemed like I hadn't been away.

With the Watergate indictment returned and the defendants arraigned, I had to seek additional evidence for the jury that would try the cover-up case. This meant finding everything possible that related to the obstruction-of-justice charges. The defendants were entitled to this. It was the prosecution's responsibility to give the judge and jury all facts that had any bearing on their guilt or innocence.

By this time I had sufficient information, primarily from the testimonies of those who had plea bargained. I felt sure these facts would be substantiated on tape recordings of conversations that took place at the White House. The voices would speak for themselves, louder than any other testimony.

But these tapes were still locked up in the White House,

despite our repeated requests for them.

On March 12, 1974, I wrote Nixon's lawyer, James St. Clair, requesting the tapes, again emphasizing their importance and adding that a response was needed by March 19.

His reply followed a familiar pattern: ". . . your request is under active consideration . . ."

A short time later White House "spokesmen" told the news media that the president had turned over "all relevant material" I had requested.

I was shocked. Had the president and his staff become so defensive that they had left the bounds of reality? More likely, I felt, they had reached a stage of desperation where no holds were barred.

I could not believe Richard Nixon was deliberately attempting to subvert the trust placed in him as chief executive. Instead, I was coming to believe that he and his intimates were suffering a paranoia, convinced that they, better than anyone else, knew what was best for the nation. In the pursuit of it they seemed to feel above the checks and balances of our constitutional government.

I had no recourse but to issue a public statement to counteract the White House's announcement that they had turned over "all relevant material." If our requests for the tapes were not met, I asserted, we would have no choice but to issue a subpoena in accordance with the earlier agreement made between the president and myself when I took the job as special prosecutor.

I warned James St. Clair in a letter that I would apply to Judge Sirica for a trial subpoena on Tuesday, April 16. Late the afternoon of the fifteenth, I received a letter from him, but no hint of compliance.

On April 16, we asked Judge Sirica to direct the president to turn over tape recordings and documents relating to sixty-four conversations between President Nixon and four of his former top aides: John Dean, Bob Haldeman, John Ehrlichman, and Charles Colson.

A few days later the House Judiciary Committee issued a

subpoena for the same materials. The president was to comply by April 30. On the night of April 29, President Nixon answered the subpoena on national television.

"And my actions and reactions as demonstrated on the tapes that follow that date (March 21, 1973), show clearly that I did not intend the further payment to Hunt or anyone else be made."

But on March 21, 1973, he had said privately to Dean: "That's why for your immediate thing, you've got no choice with Hunt but the hundred and twenty thousand dollars or whatever it is. Would you agree that that's a buy-time thing, you better ---- well get that done, but fast?" He had said that in the same Oval Office from which he now addressed the American people.

Nixon said he would make transcripts of the subpoenaed tapes available. ". . . these transcripts will show that what I have stated from the beginning to be the truth has been the truth . . ."

As I listened to these words I wondered just how much editing would be done on the transcripts. My concern was justified when we received them. Some of the recordings of conversations we already possessed were so edited and distorted in the transcripts that we had no confidence in the remainder.

Time and again we fought for the tapes—even paring the figure from sixty-four to just eighteen—but the White House continued to refuse to release them. It was clear to us that they considered these eighteen tapes very incriminating. The president, said the White House, would withhold them as a matter of "executive privilege."

A hearing was held before Judge John Sirica, and he sustained my subpoena for release of the tapes.

The White House appealed.

And now we faced another crisis.

Time was critical. The White House was stalling; any delay at all would be in its favor. Without this vital evidence the case could not proceed effectively.

Normally, the United States Circuit Court of Appeals would be the next intermediate court. But what if the White House again appealed? This would be another impediment. The only answer I saw was to leapfrog this intermediate court and go directly to the Supreme Court, a move permitted only twice in recent decades. Our timetable required that this be accomplished promptly so that the Supreme Court could hear and decide the case before its summer adjournment.

Everything now balanced on this stratagem. Would the Supreme Court grant us this right? Without it the tapes would remain secret and the Watergate case would be closed.

We filed our petition with the Supreme Court and anxiously awaited the answer.

19
End of a Nightmare

Finally it came. The Supreme Court would hear our case! They would decide whether or not the president could keep the tapes from us because of "executive privilege."

Monday, July 8, 1974, dawned hot and muggy, a typical summer day in the capital.

As our group emerged from our car in front of the marble-columned Supreme Court building on Independence Avenue, we were swamped by newspeople. Along with them was a crowd of several hundred young people, many shouting encouragement. Some with sleeping bags had been waiting outside the building since Saturday night.

I was nervous, "fractious" as we say in Texas . . . an itching eagerness for the action to begin.

"Ninety degrees already and it's not ten o'clock," someone said.

An aide whispered: "Look who's sitting next to Mrs. Jaworski!" I glanced over the heads of the milling crowd. Jeannette was sitting next to H.R. Haldeman, his hair much longer than the crew cut he had worn before resigning the year before. Seated on the other side was my son, Joseph, now thirty-nine, partner in another large Houston law firm and a trial lawyer in his own right.

As my counsel, Philip Lacovara, and I took seats at the long table at the front of the courtroom I looked up at the nine empty chairs behind the bench awaiting the Supreme Court justices. Even the dark wood emitted strength.

I glanced around the massive courtroom. I had previously argued several cases before this Court and, as always, was struck by the vast dignity of this room. It was truly a place where the honor of the Republic reposed. The double row of pillars flanking each side of the room apeared capable of supporting every good intention every administration had entertained.

"*Oyez! Oyez! Oyez!*" the marshal was calling the Court into session—and my nervousness disappeared. From behind heavy burgundy draperies emerged the eight black-robed justices. The ninth justice, William Rehnquist, had disqualified himself from the case because he had served as assistant attorney general under John Mitchell.

As I sat there I thought how all these months it had been like walking a tightrope, hoping I wouldn't slip, hoping someone else wouldn't make me slip, knowing that a slip could cost it all.

The timing had been everything, I thought. An unseen hand had arranged it so that even the grinding frustrations had played their part in delaying or hastening the action so all of us at this precise moment had reached this rendezvous with history.

The preliminaries were over and I was on my feet facing the justices. In my allotted hour they stopped me 115 times with questions. During my presentation I struck a blow at the often-argued "executive privilege," since in this instance it was a shield for wrongdoing, and not a safeguard for military or diplomatic secrets.

St. Clair argued that the Court had no right to rule on the

case, because it was a political procedure from which the Court was excluded. The House Judiciary Committee's impeachment inquiry was political, he said. He wound up by saying that the Court should stay its hand until after the impeachment hearing had run its course. ". . . those are political decisions being made, they should not bear the burden, either way, of a judicial decision."

A justice answered: "Well, under that theory, all the criminal trials that are going on should stop then."

Soon the time was up. Now the justices would go into their deliberations. As I walked out of the Court I remembered what Justice William O. Douglas had said when I had emphasized that St. Clair's briefs had insisted only the president was the proper one to interpret the Constitution on executive privilege.

Justice Douglas had leaned forward and said, "Well, we start with a Constitution that does not contain the words *executive privilege*—is that right?"

"That is right, sir," I had said, thinking how those two words had been misappropriated by our nation's chief executive.

Justice Douglas had answered, "So why don't we go on from there. . . ."

I found myself silently praying that God's will would prevail in the deliberations of the justices as we stepped out into the sunlight.

The roar from the crowd when they saw us was deafening. A few people were knocked down in the crush. Finally, we got into our car, and one of my staff said, "Law students . . . 90 percent of those people are law students."

In the meantime the House Judiciary Committee had gone ahead and would begin holding public hearings on July 24. The committee was prepared to vote on a resolution or resolutions of impeachment without benefit of additional information.

Most of us felt that the committee's case would be weakened without the eighteen tapes I was trying to get. But the pressures on them to begin the hearings had been tremendous, and they were going ahead.

On July 23, the day before the committee's hearings were to start, we were notified that the Supreme Court would render its decision at 9:30 A.M. the next morning.

The crowd outside the Supreme Court Building that hot and humid morning was larger and louder than before. Inside the packed hall the tension was electric. I had reason to believe that Nixon was confident that his assertion of executive privilege would prevail.

We would soon know.

The marshal cried out his ancient command, the draperies parted, and the eight justices solemnly took their seats. For some reason I relaxed. I had rested everything in the hands of God. There was nothing more I could do.

Chief Justice Warren Burger began reading from the Court's opinion in an assured manner.

The case, he said, had satisfied all the legal requirements to appear before the Court. Congress, he said, had vested in the attorney general the power to conduct the criminal litigation of the United States Government, and the power to appoint subordinate officers to assist him in this. The attorney general had delegated this authority to a special prosecutor, and the special prosecutor had explicit power to contest the argument of executive privilege in seeking evidence deemed relevant to the performance of these duties.

He went on to point out that our office had come up with sufficient evidence to justify a subpoena.

Now the chief justice took a longer pause than usual, as if preparing to explain the heart of the matter.

"We turn to the claim that the subpoena should be quashed because it demands confidential conversations between a president and his close advisers that it would be inconsistent with the public interest to produce."

He pointed out that though each branch of the government must initially interpret the Constitution, it has been historically reaffirmed that "it is emphatically the province and duty of the Judicial Department to say what the law is.

He continued, his voice reaching every corner of the hall, his listeners rapt.

"We conclude that . . . the ground for asserting privilege as to subpoenaed materials cannot prevail over the fundamental demands of due process of law. On the basis of our examination of the records . . . we affirm the order of the District Court that the subpoenaed material is to be transmitted to that court. . . ."

We had won!

And then came the information I had so much wanted to hear: the holding of the Court was unanimous!

Court was adjourned, the justices disappeared behind the heavy draperies, and the room exploded into near pandemonium. What the Supreme Court of the United States had said to the president was this: The rule of law—the spirit of constitutionalism—belongs to the people. It excludes none, and it exempts none.

After making our way through a mass of people offering congratulations, and newsmen shouting questions, we got into the car and I fell back in the seat, quietly giving thanks.

The unanimous holding, I was convinced, had saved the country from an even more terrible trauma than it was already experiencing.

Had we lost the Supreme Court case, Watergate would have been at an end.

Had the White House not been required to deliver the tape recordings, the case would have been dismissed.

And the unanimous decision of the High Court was of extreme importance. President Nixon had hinted that if the Court cast a divided vote, he might not comply with the order to deliver the tapes.

Among the tape recordings turned over to us, which we passed on to the House Judiciary Committee, was a conversation that had taken place June 23, 1972, only six days after the Watergate break-in. It showed that the president was fully advised of the break-in, that he had participated in plans to cover it up, that he had conspired along with others to obstruct justice, and that he had sought to have the FBI called off the case and turn it over to the CIA to be buried under the guise of national security.

As I listened to his conversation with Bob Haldeman I remembered President Nixon's face only three months earlier when he had addressed the people of the United States from the Oval Office on April 23. He had said that "The full resources of the FBI and the Justice Department were used to investigate the incident thoroughly."

And yet on these tapes I heard President Nixon and Haldeman discussing ways to quash the FBI investigation of Watergate, only six days after the break-in.

". . . the FBI is not under control," Haldeman had reported to Nixon. "Because Gray (the acting FBI director) doesn't exactly know how to control them. And they have, their investigation is now leading into some productive areas."

After enumerating some of those areas, he stated Attorney General John Mitchell's recommendation: to have someone "call Pat Gray and just say, 'Stay the ---- out of this business here. We don't want you to go any further on it' . . ."

Obviously when Nixon made that address in April he had never expected to reveal anything more than his highly edited transcripts.

Now the tapes had been exposed for all to hear and judge. Nixon and his aides would answer "to God, to history, and to our conscience" for the way in which they had used their last years in the White House.

Once the June 23 tape and other startling information reached the Judiciary Committee and the nation, President Nixon resigned and the nation was spared further trauma in the Watergate matter.

Some weeks later on Sunday morning, September 8, 1974, Jeannette and I were in our apartment preparing to attend church services at the National Presbyterian Church on Nebraska Avenue, which was some distance away.

We had become friendly with a young Jewish man who had

accompanied us to church several previous Sundays, and he had planned to come by our apartment around 10:30 A.M. so we would ride together to the eleven o'clock service.

At 9:30 A.M. the telephone rang. It was Phillip Buchen, President Ford's counsel, calling to tell me that the president had decided to pardon Richard Nixon. At 11:00 A.M. that morning he would appear on television to disclose his decision to the nation.

We decided to go on to church anyway. However, I left the conversation up to Jeannette and our friend. I could not get my mind off the news I had just heard.

The pardon had come as no real surprise to me. There had been some discussion between President Ford and the news media on several prior occasions about the possibility of the president's taking this action. To be prepared I had studied the legal issues to determine whether it was possible and if it could be challenged. I had learned that the pardoning power of the United States president under the Constitution was not subject to question. He could pardon for a good reason, or no reason at all.

However, as we drove to the church the impact of the pardon became stronger with each passing moment.

The long nightmare had ended. Now the cover-up trial of Mitchell, Haldeman, Ehrlichman, and the others could proceed without any interference.

I had arranged for my assistant, Jim Neal, to head the prosecution, and now we were marking time, waiting for the case to be called. The remaining work of the special prosecutor's office was relatively minor; there were a few campaign contribution violations to be cleaned up and not much more. To me, everything would now be an anticlimax. It would soon be time to return home to Texas.

As we stepped into the sanctuary, the usher met us and took us to our seats. I settled down in the pew and thought about how just seven months ago in another church I had watched a United States president proudly walk in and join the congregation in prayer.

Now I felt only pity and compassion for the man and his family, and I found myself praying that he and his loved ones would be given the strength to face the days ahead.

The organ prelude ended and someone began speaking from the pulpit, but I wasn't listening. Perhaps I was not prepared to adjust myself to the sudden ending of this tragic drama. I was not concentrating on the service, the lesson, or the sermon. Every few minutes I would lapse into silent prayer, thanking God for ending Wategate without serious harm to the country. It turned out to be my own private hour of worship in silent communication with a benevolent Father who had again allowed his blessings to shine on our nation.

20
In God We Trust

It was time to go home.

I watched the landmarks of the capital sparkle in the sun as our plane lifted from Washington's airport. Below was the dome of the Jefferson Memorial, the marble facets of the Lincoln Memorial, and the soaring spire of the Washington Monument, all symbols to me of great and honorable men who served our nation in forging a government with sinews of law that hold it together.

These men would have been stunned by Watergate. But they would also have been proud of the judiciary they created and maintained. There was a trial judge who did not accept distortions of the truth. There was an appellate court that acted decisively to meet the president's first challenge of opposing the release of the tapes. The same trial court and appellate court decided without delay that a crucial grand jury report should be transmitted to the House Judiciary Committee. And that trial court overruled the president's claim of executive privilege in response to a subpoena involving criminal wrongdoing. In the end, the Supreme Court, with bold dispatch, laid to rest the troublesome problems that beset the nation.

Suppose these individuals and courts had not measured up courageously and judiciously to the traumatic issues? The result would have been a chapter in our history books charging that our courts were ineffective. Respect for the administration of justice at a time when suspicion lurked in the minds of the young would have received a serious setback. And there would have been no end to the nation's ordeal. The wounds of doubt and disillusionment might never have healed.

From Watergate we learned what generations of Americans before us have known: our Constitution works. And during the ordeal it was interpreted again to reaffirm the truth that no one—absolutely no one—is above the law.

Still fresh on my mind was the sadness of seeing men, who once had fame in their hands, sinking into infamy. These men had forgotten Alexander Pope's words: "Unblemished, let me live or die unknown. Give me an honest fame or give me none."

As our plane wheeled toward the southwest I wondered: Could God have stopped Watergate from happening? Of course, just as he could have altered its course at any minute.

To me there is only one logical explanation for Watergate's occurring with God's awareness. I think that the Special Prosecution Force Report states it quite clearly:

Many of the Watergate phenomena had their historical precedents. Many had grown with no deterrence from other branches of government. Others had grown without questions from the people and from the press. . . . As with any coalescing of activities that lead to a national crisis, so, too, did Watergate grow from historical roots that presaged abuses of institutional power.

So have other evils grown throughout history. I saw the rise of the Ku Klux Klan in my own county to where every elected post but one in my community was held by a Klan member. I saw the results of such an insidious growth of power in Germany, all of it happening because of wrong dreams and aspirations. Right and wrong had been forgotten. Little evils were permitted to grow into great evils, small sins to escalate into big sins.

Nothing surprised me more than the attitude of a segment of citizens who could not be bothered by the revelations of this great trauma. With a wave of their arm or a shrug of the shoulders, they would remark, "It has been going on for a long time." Or, "It did not begin with Watergate."

How long these practices may have been going on—or whether such perfidy was greater or lesser or equal to Watergate—is not even a mitigating circumstance. The question is: Why were these instances not brought to light? Why were the offenders not called to an accounting for their wrongs?

The answer would have to be that they were condoned, and thus permitted to serve as a spawning ground for subsequent misdeeds, either because of a lack of vigilance or because of indolence in attending to them. The thought of the evils that might have crept into government if these men had not been held accountable is devastating.

But must we all not stand accountable with them as we watch the waning of morality in our country? We see the growth of white-collar crime in which employees cheat employers and vice versa, the tragedy of upper-and middle-income people bilking insurance companies with fraudulent claims and avoiding income taxes, and news of high-level government officials caught red-handed in payoff schemes.

To combat vice, massive government investigations are launched, new legislation is introduced, and at election time the rascals usually are voted out.

And yet, it seems to go on and on . . .

I see only one answer to it all: that those who profess a

religious faith rededicate themselves to its principles. I believe religion played a vital part in the formation of America.

Time and again through history our religious foundations have been severely challenged. I believe the church and the power of prayer were put to their severest test during the Civil War. It was during this time that Abraham Lincoln said: "Blessed be God, Who, in this our great trial, giveth us the Churches."

My concern now is that we are failing the Almighty.

I have the strongest faith in our religious institutions, and I would like to believe that they will offer the leadership to meet the challenges our society faces. But I have heard it said that little can be expected from the church because its influence is waning.

The well-known writer, James J. Kilpatrick, in pointing to the disintegration of the community refers to "the steady erosion of forces that once were powerful." The first force under erosion he named was the church.

And so we ask: Who is the church? It is ordinary people who assemble together in the name of God. But the church cannot fulfill its God-given responsibilities without a militant membership—militant in supporting the church with worldly means as well as assisting its pastors in fervently carrying on its work.

Sadly, I feel that in general our churches today are weak. And this weakness lies not just in diminishing membership rolls among the major denominations, but stems from the apathy of those on the rolls. To attend church on Sundays is commendable. But to sit in the pew for an hour of worship and do no more than that for God's Kingdom and his righteousness can hardly lay up treasures in heaven.

I often think how lonely and helpless some ministers must feel after the Sunday services. The sanctuary is filled, and the minister ponders what great work for the Lord these many individuals could do. But he neither hears from them nor sees them again until some other Sunday—in many cases not until the next Christmas or Easter, or when he is called to conduct the funeral of one of their loved ones.

I thought of Jesus as he went through his ordeal of suffering in the Garden of Gethsemane, and how, when he looked to his disciples for comfort and support, he found them all asleep.

Too often, when the church needs us, when our country needs us, we are asleep. *How long will it take,* I wondered, *before enough of us awaken?* I shuddered as I thought of another nation of people who awakened too late, after a madman had taken power.

We have been given great blessings. Our land is one of the great natural resources. We have magnificent cities and fertile fields and a form of government that is second to none on the globe. We are unmatched in technological advancements. We have the capacity for world leadership. But in the midst of all this abundance are the signs of decay: the resurgence of race hatred and civil disorder, the flagrant violation of our country's laws, and an obsession with self-indulgence and easy morals.

DeTocqueville's challenge rings out to us today: "If America ever ceases to be good, it will cease to be great."

In our precious land, moral decay must not gain a foothold. If it does, it may spread like a cancerous growth.

The antidote? The church militant.

Whither goest thou?

21
For All That Has Been . . .
And to All That Shall Be

It had started out as a most pleasant evening.

Jeannette and I were returning home from hearing the Houston Symphony that misty December night in 1979. As we drove through the dark in the warm afterglow that comes from hearing beautiful music, I was thinking of this book on which I had been working. Earlier in the day I had finished writing about my grandson Mike's death, and it had brought back bittersweet memories from seven years ago.

The tires sang on the wet pavement; soon we had reached our street and were turning into our drive when Jeannette exclaimed: "Oh, Joanie is here." Our eldest daughter's car was parked in the driveway.

After stepping out of the car we quickly walked to the door. It opened, and Joanie stepped out, her face tear-stained and pale. She embraced each of us, then said quietly, "David is dead."

Dazed, we stood frozen in shock for a few moments, then

turned to our car and drove to the home of his parents, our daughter, Claire, and her husband, Bob.

We learned that it had happened in Austin where the University of Texas is located. David had been riding home as a passenger on the rear of a motorcycle. As they reached a corner, a befuddled motorist, traveling against a traffic light turned into the motorcycle. The cycle driver survived with a broken leg and bruises, but David's skull was crushed.

"David died almost instantly," Joanie said.

There was no doubt that each of us had the same thought: he died much the same way Mike had.

None of us could sleep that night as we each retreated into our own grief. I couldn't believe it. David, only twenty-two and preparing to complete his senior year at the University of Texas!

I sat there looking out into space remembering when we had last seen our grandson. He and his family had spent Thanksgiving Day with us at the ranch just a few days ago. David had accompanied me in the jeep back into the hills to cut up dead trees and stack some firewood. As usual, we had a good time talking. As we bounced along he told me about the fun he and his younger brothers, twenty-one-year-old Robert and nineteen-year-old John, had had earlier that day.

"We found a terrific spot up at Horseshoe Bend," he had grinned. "You know the place, with that big rock?"

I nodded. It was a beautiful glade surrounded by Spanish oaks. I remembered a lovely wild holly bush that grew there.

"We three must have spent an hour just sitting and gabbing on that big old rock," he chuckled.

"What did you talk about?" I knew the three brothers were very close.

"Oh," he laughed, throwing back his head, "we talked about which one of us would get married first." He smiled. "We decided it would be Robert."

Yes, I thought now as I gazed into the night, it would be Robert. He was now the oldest Draper boy. As the night deepened, so did my thoughts.

I had become reconciled to Mike's death. Should I reexamine this? I wondered. Was the peace of mind I seemed to have achieved disquieted in the wake of this new tragedy?

David's funeral was held at the Memorial Drive Presbyterian Church in Houston, which the Draper family attended and where Claire serves as an elder. Its former pastor, Dr. Robert R. Ball, who knew David quite well, had flown in from California. After the church's resident pastor, Dr. James A. Wharton, opened the services, Dr. Ball gave the message.

I had expected the usual funeral services when Dr. Ball announced that this would be "a celebration of thanksgiving and praise for the life of David Elliott Draper."

Celebration? It didn't seem fitting.

But as he proceeded I began to understand. He called David "Eli," a nickname his close friends had given him. As Dr. Ball continued, I became aware that Eli had been his close friend.

"When Eli and I knew each other I was a preacher, but he never held that against me," he said.

"He acknowledged that I was a human being by letting me know him as a human being also. He asked me honest questions about what I saw when I looked at life, and then he invited me to come in and walk around inside *his* life.

"He was just as honest about his fears and his spots of vulnerability as he was about his dreams and his accomplishments," continued Dr. Ball. "One time he even told me he loved me. And I loved him."

Had I told David that I loved him? I wondered. I couldn't remember that I had. I hoped I had done so.

"Last night," the minister said, "it came to me how uniquely rare it is to have contact with another human being—one who truly treats you as an equal. And Eli did that for me. Those moments are so precious, so full of life, so much what life at its best is meant to be that when they are happening to you, you have the impulse to take off your shoes—for you are standing on holy ground. Somehow you realize that you are living at that moment in the presence of God."

I thought back to such moments of closeness with my family. I realized that such interludes were the Lord's precious gifts.

"Paul knew that experience," continued Dr. Ball, describing the apostle's writing from a Roman prison to his dear friends in Philippi. "As he wrote, he was well aware that he would probably never see them again on this earth and yet, Paul, in that letter, could not find enough ways in which to express the joy he was feeling. And he fell all over himself telling the Philippians how grateful he was for their friendship. He was grateful *for* them but he was grateful *to* God because he was so very much aware that God is the one who gives life, and life's deepest meaning is friendship. . . .

"The people at Philippi were Paul's spiritual children," Dr. Ball said. "He had reared them and nurtured them, but he was more than their father because they had shared their lives with him and he had shared his with them, as equals. Now, as he sat there in prison and realized that he would probably not see them again, he felt no bitterness or self-pity for he understood that this gift of love and friendship is never our possession. But it is indeed a freely given gracious gift. Though the immediacy of that friendship was probably over, Paul was saying that the experience of it and the reality of it would be a joy forever.

"So it is in our feelings for Eli," continued the minister, "we would not ask to be spared the agony and the misery of this moment at the cost of having never known and loved him."

As I sat there in the pew, my mind riveted to his every word, I found myself admitting that I would accept all the sorrow in my heart for the joy of knowing and loving David and Mike. I found myself quietly thanking God for the years I had with them.

Dr. Ball continued, "Human life according to the Scriptures is not a matter of ever arriving somewhere, but it is a matter of being on the road, being on the way, a matter of *becoming*.

". . . somehow, someway, the message had gotten through to Eli that life is given to be lived, and so he continually took it out in the marketplace and lived it. The way Jesus Christ teaches us to measure the meaning of life, the life that Eli lived was full of meaning."

Dr. Ball's voice rose and I found myself sharing his exuberance. This truly *was* a celebration.

"It really seems that we are never ready for the end of anything that is precious to us," he said. "In our fear we always seem to feel that what we have in our hands is surely better than what is to be. This is in spite of the fact that Jesus Christ continually comes at us with his surprise endings, which strikes me as the one most consistent theme running through all of his parables.

"I don't have any explanation for why tragedies such as this occur," said Dr. Ball, looking from one to another of us, "and I cannot claim any special wisdom as to how it is all going to turn out. But as a disciple of Jesus Christ, it is my hunch that Eli, who treated me and a lot of other human beings as equals, was right at the center of what it's all about . . . and still is . . . and always will be."

He paused for a moment, then concluded: "As Dag Hammarskjold said: 'For all that has been, thanks. To all that shall be, yes.' "

We buried David in the Memorial Oaks Cemetery next to Mike.

After the funeral Jeannette and I visited with Claire and Bob, David's parents, and then headed for the ranch.

As the sparse countryside of south central Texas rolled past us I kept thinking about Dr. Ball's message. David had viewed us all as equal, saints and sinners, princes and serfs, intellectuals and illiterates. He made no exceptions. As I turned the powerful message over and over in my mind I realized that this is precisely what Christ taught us. I had to admit that my grandson, as a young man, had learned something that I, as an old man, had not yet really learned in its most fundamental sense.

I thought back on all I had come up against through the years, those who condemned me for defending Jordan Scott, the men and women in Germany blinded to God, the errant state governor, the misguided president and his staff.

All of us are equal in the Lord's eyes, all of us in one way or another are sinners. Each of us is a human being making his way through life to be judged in the end only by God, not man.

The next morning at the ranch dawned crisp and clear. Hoarfrost sparkled on the grass. I put on an old jacket and went back to where David and I had last worked and continued the job we had started. It seemed only right.

A large, fallen Spanish oak had to be cut up. Now I worked alone. But in a way I wasn't alone. David and Mike were both with me as I labored there in the little clearing and then stacked the wood.

I found myself drawn to the little grove at Horseshoe Bend, which David had told me about. I drove over to where his brother, John, had told me it was and switched off the jeep's engine. The quiet was broken only by the low hum of wind through the Spanish oaks.

I got out of the jeep and walked into the glade. There was the big rock that only a short time ago had rung to the enthusiastic voices of three brothers.

As they had laughed and talked about their future none of them had known that very shortly Robert and John would be at their brother's funeral, paying tribute to him in choked-up voices and thanking God for the years that he had given them together.

I sat down on the rock, listening to the wind and looking up into the tree-framed sky, remembering how David had helped renew my awareness of life in all its beauty. And the mystery of the adventure on which we all are embarked became clearer to me.

I remembered the bright hope in my father's eyes as he spoke of the many mansions that Jesus had prepared. Now, Mike and David were on that same adventure. How unreasonable, I thought, that we who are left insist that our loved ones embark on this adventure in order of their ages. In his great plan, the Lord has his own timetable, which far surpasses our feeble understanding.

215

Later, David's brother Robert and I returned to the little grove at Horseshoe Bend and explored the work needed to clear and groom it. Then I took the remaining three horseshoes with the brothers' names from the toolhouse door, and Robert and I nailed them to a tree in the glade. Robert and John with the help of their parents carefully groomed the site planting various species of cacti from different parts of the ranch, transforming the spot into a beautifully landscaped memorial.

Horseshoe Bend, dedicated to David, and Swamp Fox's glade, dedicated to Mike, have become shrines for our family, which we often visit. They are not memorials to the dead but victorious affirmations of the living.

As the philosopher, Tagore, said, "death is not extinguishing the light, it is only putting out the lamp because the dawn has come."

Instead of questioning God's purposes, I now accept them in terms of his plan for us all. Did he not take his Son at an early age, too?

My children and grandchildren have bequeathed to me a legacy of rich and radiant memories that become more precious with each passing year.

Now as I enter my seventy-fifth year, I know there will be more crossroads to come. With the Lord's guidance and support, I will do my best to meet them. And whatever happens, I can only pray:

"For all that has been, thanks. To all that shall be, yes."